THOUGHTS TO MEDITATE ON
52 Exercises For Inner
Peace And Tranquility

I0162377

Kennard Ramphal

MiddleRoad | Publishers

Making Literature see the light of day

Library and Archives Canada Cataloguing in Publication
Ramphal, Kennard, Author
*Thoughts To Meditate On/ 52 Exercises For A Year Of Inner
Peace And Tranquility*

ISBN 978-1-990765-65-0 (paperback)
Editor: Ken Puddicombe www.kenpud.wordpress.com

Cover Design: Kathryn Lagerquist
Kathryn.lagerquist@gmail.com

Praise for
THOUGHTS TO MEDITATE ON
52 Exercises For Inner Peace
And Tranquillity

"These treatises are motivational and instructional—they give the reader reassurance in tackling life's obstacles that test our strength, patience and resilience."

—Frank Mohan MD, FCFP (LM)—

Author: *Love Has Two Moons And Other Stories*

"Dr. Kennard Ramphal, or "Dr. Ken" as many of us affectionately know him, is a master of both the written and spoken word. His love of God and his fellow man are skillfully woven into short meditative reflections on the universal truths of the human experience with the unique ability to convey an august sense of life experience and a down-to-earth pragmatism few can match but all can relate to."

—Daniel P. Stewart—

Ed.D, Curriculum and Teaching

MA, Humanities

"Dr. Ken Ramphal's heartfelt and practical meditations provide insights into the human condition while offering sound guidance for coping with everyday life. His meditations inspire me and give me hope for the future. His stories in all of his works are a joy to read!"

—Tammy L. Stewart, MLS—

Dean of Learning Resources and Academic Librarian

Sandhills Community College

"...heartfelt and deeply moving, based on life's experiences...easily defined as either meditations or medications for the soul as they have brought me strength and restoration in times when it was much needed. I reference them often as they provide solid practical advice in many circumstances."

—Benjamin P. Cribb, B.Sc. EET—

Product Safety and Electrical Engineer

ALSO BY KENNARD RAMPHAL

- *Seeram's Illusions*
- *Teacher Ram's Fascination With Fire*
- *Dilchand Joins The Army*
- *Escape To The Canadian Jungle*
- *Ramlall's Strange Courtship and Wedding*
- *Slippery Ochro (3rd Prize Guyana Prize For Literature: Fiction 2023)*

Co Author:
- *Imprints In Life's Journey* (with Barbara Verasami and Dwarka Ramphal)
- *Snapshots Of Our Lives* (with Ram Jagessar and Roop Misir)

"If you change the way you look at things, the things you look at change."

—Wayne Dyer—
1940-2015
Internationally renowned author and speaker in the fields of self-development and spiritual growth.

DEDICATION

To my wife Orna, my children and their spouses, and my grandchildren—Maya, Marisa, Seth, Sasha and Basil.

ACKNOWLEDGMENTS

Thanks to my publisher, Ken Puddicombe, owner of MiddleRoad Publishers, for his rigorous editing. Members of the Carican group of writers, Dr. Harry Persaud, Dr. Roop Misir, Dr. Rosetta Khalideen, and Dr. Frank Mohan read and edited each passage in the book, and offered valuable suggestions. The book is better for their input.

My wife, Orna, my children, Savita, Yogita and Rajendra, and my sons-in-law, Max Naraine and Simon Eberlie were always there with their support and encouragement. One of the least expected and most welcome source of support has come from my two eldest grand-daughters, Maya and Marisa. I can remember holding them in my arms just the other day, and suddenly they are reading my book and offering me advice like, "Consider moving this paragraph to the first page."

I thank members of the New Millenium ministry, founded by my brother, Dr. Dwarka Ramphal, who listened to modified versions of the meditations and who advised me to publish and share them with a wider audience.

Many thanks to Barb Scott and Michael Laframboise who read and edited each passage and urged me to continue writing.

Col. Fabie Liverpool, with whom I served in the Guyana Defence Force, constantly supported my writing and urged me, "Do not let your stories and your thoughts die with you."

Lastly, and most important, thanks to all my readers out there who have given me positive feedback on my writing. Your appreciation and support mean a great deal to me.

Table of Contents

PREFACE

I have read many self-help books, and they have helped me immensely. I am no expert in psychology or spirituality, but I would like to share what I've learnt from these books and from my life-long experiences. Most of the passages are interrelated and there are necessarily some overlaps between meditations.

My suggestion is that you take a few minutes each day, and read and meditate on one section every week. Over time, they will become part of your thinking, and of your life.

My earnest hope is that you will find reading these passages as helpful as I did in writing them.

Kennard Ramphal

INTRODUCTION

Dr. Kennard Ramphal's book, *THOUGHTS TO MEDITATE ON explores* deep and inspiring allegorical stories of the human attempts to find higher meanings in life. He has developed unique ways of expressing simple but profound thoughts by many world thinkers, adding his personal interpretations and experiences to life's lessons. Dr. Ramphal has painted a colourful picture, and gives new perspectives to the art of living. He has given fresh meanings to the human condition and suggests ways of combatting depression and unhappiness. This has been the recurrent theme throughout the book.

The central message of *THOUGHTS TO MEDITATE ON* is a powerful re-evaluation of the human need to find happiness and contentment in life. Dr. Ramphal encourages his readers to follow their hearts in order to find a greater purpose in life. He observes that there is an apparent shifting downwards of spirituality and moral values in the world at the current time, with implications of a deterioration and degradation of society.

Dr. Ramphal examines some of the maladies of modern societal norms and the need to rebalance 'old' philosophical and religious wisdom with 'new' scientific knowledge into a composite whole. In this way, we learn from the past as we forge ahead into a more resilient and brighter future.

Dr. Ramphal made references in his meditation on "Freedom" that we should strive not only for physical freedom but also for "...freedom from emotional and psychological conditionings which bind us to the status quo...". He envisions that we should fulfill our "need for love and self-respect" through self-discovery, and to share these qualities with fellow humans.

Formerly a long-term educator in Metropolitan Toronto, Dr. Ramphal demonstrates that our educational system somewhat curtails "intellectual freedom" and could be seen as "cages for mind control," clearly citing that one should exercise freedom of thought at all times, as he quotes from the scriptures: "...know the truth and the truth shall set you free."

The author, in his piece "You are only Human" entreats that as humans, we must not forget our limitations; we should strive to be "humble and simple" in our dispositions, reminding us that no one lives forever. Therefore, learn to forgive oneself and whenever depressed, sad or angry "remember your humanity."

The profundity and sophistication of Dr. Ramphal's thinking is aptly described in his chapter on "The Ego vs Self." He stresses that we must learn to distinguish between our "... outer identity from our true Self existing within the Higher Consciousness," and reminds us that the Soul is "immune to criticism, and is without fear and prejudice." With regards to the true *Self*, he quotes from Dr. Deepak Chopra: "And yet it is humble and feels superior to no one, because it recognizes that everyone else is the same *Self*, the same spirit in different disguises." The author explains that the Ego, on the other hand is not who you really are; your "self-image is a mask hiding you from your true identity."

I first met Dr. Kennard Ramphal about two decades ago, when we co-authored a book of poetry. Ever since, he has played an integral part in my writing experience, as he continues to inspire and motivate me to surge ahead in my writings. Like Dr. Ramphal, I have also pursued the "big questions" of life—who are we, why we are here and what could be some of the reasons for our existence at this time and in this geography. Without being over teleological, we seek to understand some of the purposes for our *Beings*. I could not find a more suitable candidate in such a pursuit than Ken Ramphal. He is gifted with a sharp wit but more importantly, he has been smitten by the joy of writing, always searching for higher meanings within the context of organization and order. I describe Kennard as a wonderful human being, rich in experiences of life and a gentle soul. I could not be more fortunate to call him my friend.

—Harry Persaud Ph.D. (Anthropology)—

Author: *The River Crossing: A Path to Self-Discovery*

Martial Artist,

Student of Eastern Philosophy.

1 A JOURNEY OF A THOUSAND MILES

The saying, *A journey of a thousand miles begins with a single step,* is attributed to the Chinese philosopher, Lao Tzi.

If you have a difficult, long and tedious task to perform, just begin the task, even if you spend just a few minutes on it. You will be surprised at how much you can achieve by expending a few minutes a day on a task.

The popular maxim, *A job once begun, is half done*, also has a great deal of merit.

It is easy and tempting to procrastinate. Furthermore, the more you procrastinate, the easier it will be for you to continue procrastinating, making it more and more difficult to begin the task on hand. If you don't begin the task, the job will never get done, because it has been scientifically proven that no job, which has not been started, has ever been completed.

In the comedy, *Twelfth Night,* Shakespeare reminded us that procrastination leads to no rewards when he wrote, "In delay, there lies no plenty."

It is crucial to focus on the step you are taking now, instead of dwelling on the steps that you have already taken, or looking ahead, and dreading the steps that you have to take.

If you look back, you're likely to dwell on the many missteps you took during your journey, and regret that you did not take the many shortcuts that were available. Hindsight is always 20/20. You are also likely to stumble if you focus on the past.

And if you look at all the steps you must take to reach your destination, you may be daunted by the impending difficulties.

But if you focus on the one step you are taking at the present moment, the task becomes manageable.

Many people have monumental achievements simply by focusing on one task at a time. For example, Joseph Payeng, from Assam, India, was alarmed by the erosion on the island on which he was living, and planted a tree every day for 40 years. The forest he planted now covers 1,360 acres, and is home to many tigers and elephants, among other animals.

Just imagine! A single tree every day for 40 years! Did Joseph Payeng look back and say, I have already planted twenty trees, so it's time to stop. Or did he worry about the number of trees he had to plant? No! He went on to plant a SINGLE tree every day for forty years, and created a forest.

In Guyana, there is a saying, *One one dutty build dam*[1] meaning that large tasks can be accomplished by doing a little at a time. I'm certain that there are sayings in other cultures which emphasize the same concept, and we are all familiar with the saying, "It all adds up."

I am reminded of my parents' coffee farm in Canal No. 2, Guyana. Imagine almost a mile of coffee trees,

---

[1] A Lump of earth added, eventually builds a dam!

laden with ripe coffee berries. We could have looked at all the trees and berries, and declared, "It's too much to handle."

Instead, along with some laborers hired by my parents, we picked ONE berry at a time. The result was a large crop of coffee berries, which we dried before we took them to the coffee mill, and which provided an income.

At the time I am writing this, I have authored or co-authored seven books, and have the manuscript for the eighth almost ready for publication. I did not write a page every day, because on some days I had other obligations. But I wrote at least a page on most days, and surprised myself with the results.

Imagine what YOU can achieve by consistently focusing on a single task.

If you are putting off a difficult task, start now in a small way, and do a little bit at a time. You'll be surprised at the results.

NOTE: A fellow writer mentioned to me that a person has to multitask in today's world. This may be true, but even when multi-tasking, a person can do only one task at a time. That task can be accomplished more efficiently if the doer concentrates on the task in which he is engaged in the present moment.

2 LIVE FOR TODAY

Many people are so worried about what they did, or what happened in the past, and are so anxious about what may happen in the future, that they don't focus on today.

Matthew 6:31 tells us: "Therefore do not be anxious about tomorrow, for tomorrow will be anxious for itself. Sufficient for the day is its own trouble."

And Psalms 118:28 emphasizes, "Today is the day that the Lord has made; let us rejoice and be glad in it."

More recently, Eckhart Tolle, in his insightful book, *The Power of Now,* writes, "The present moment is all you will ever have."

We are also encouraged to focus on today by the famous Indian poet, Khalidasa, (5th century CE, Sanskrit poet and dramatist) who wrote a beautiful poem entitled, **Salutation to the Dawn.**

> *Look to this Day!*
>
> *For it is life, the very life of life.*
> *In its brief course lie all the verities*
> *And realities of your existence:*
> *The glory of action, the bliss of growth,*
> *The splendor of beauty.*
> *For yesterday is but a dream,*
> *And tomorrow is only a vision.*
> *But today, well lived, makes*
> *Every yesterday a dream of happiness*

And every tomorrow a vision of hope.
Look well, therefore, to this Day!

Such is the Salutation of the Dawn.

This is why many people start their days by facing the sun and welcoming the new day.

Another powerful poem, which is used in *Alcoholic Anonymous* meetings to encourage members to focus on the present, instead of dwelling on errors made in the past, or worrying about problems which the future may bring, is cited below.

YESTERDAY, TODAY AND TOMORROW

There are two days in every week about which we should not worry,

Two days which should be kept free from fear and apprehension.

One of these days is Yesterday, with its mistakes and cares,
Its faults and blunders, its aches and pains.

Yesterday has passed forever beyond our control.
All the money in the world cannot bring back Yesterday.

We cannot undo a single word we said; we can't erase a single act we performed. Yesterday is gone.

The other day that we should not worry about is Tomorrow, with its possible adversities, its burdens, its large promise and poor performance.

Tomorrow is also beyond our control.

Tomorrow's sun will rise, either in splendour, or behind a mask of clouds—but it will rise.

Until it does, we have no stake in Tomorrow, for it is as yet unborn.

This leaves only one day – Today.

Any person can only fight the battles of one day.

It's only when you or I add the burdens of those awful eternities – Yesterday and Tomorrow – that we break down.

It is not the experience of Today that drives people mad.

It is the remorse or bitterness of Yesterday, or the dread of what Tomorrow may bring.

Let us therefore live but one day at a time. (Author unknown)

Worry and anxiety have become such persistent patterns of thought in our lives, that many people find it difficult to eliminate them entirely. However, if you constantly read and meditate on the above poems and other writings on the same subject, you will find that you will gradually reduce the time you spend worrying about the past and being anxious about the future.

This will leave you more time to be grateful for your blessings. In effect, you will gradually develop new thoughts, which will replace the ones of worry and anxiety.

Don't be too hard on yourself when you find that you spend precious moments worrying and being anxious. Old habits die hard. Be aware that you are developing new habits, however slowly, and that these new habits will eventually choke out the old destructive ones.

Life will be so much more rewarding when you live one day at a time. Better still, focus on the present moment, because it is all you're guaranteed.

One method of doing this, which Tolle compares to turning base metal into gold, is this: Whenever you find yourself worrying or being anxious, do not give energy to that thought. Instead, focus on your breath, and go inside your body by feeling the energy coursing through your body from head to toe. This is the energy that is keeping you alive. Tolle calls this process *inhabiting the body*. Giving attention to this energy will increase the vibrational frequency of the energy, and you will feel more alive. You would have practised the art of alchemy—turning base metals into gold.

Remember, today is all you will ever have. When tomorrow comes, it will come as today.

As a fellow traveler, I earnestly wish you all the best TODAY.

3 ACCEPTANCE

Most of us had great expectations for ourselves when we were young. As adults, some of us may have fulfilled our dreams, but it is safe to say that many people have found themselves in situations that fall short of what they envisioned. I know that I have not even come close to achieving all the goals I set for myself when I was a youth with high ideals.

The result: many people are in a constant state of unease and dissatisfied with their present circumstances.

Deepak Chopra, a well-known self-help writer, reminds us that our bodies produce a chemical with every thought. When we think pleasing and calming thoughts, our bodies secrete chemicals like endorphins which make us feel good. However, when we harbour stressful thoughts, the natural response of the body is the production of adrenaline which prepares us for the *flight or fight* response. In our society, we do not often face immediate danger, but the body does not distinguish between real and imagined danger. The adrenaline produced by the body when no action is required, results in various illnesses.

Acceptance of the situation in which we find ourselves causes our minds and bodies to be more relaxed and results in a feeling of peace—with the world and with ourselves. In this situation, we breathe more deeply, our heart rate decreases, and our blood pressure goes down.

Along with accepting our present circumstances, it is crucial that we accept and love ourselves, regardless of all our faults, regardless of how short or how tall we are, regardless of the shapes of our noses and other body parts. Accept your body, because you are stuck with it for your entire life. This will be discussed more fully in another meditation.

In addition to accepting ourselves, it is crucial that we accept others as they are. They are part of our situation. Many relationships were damaged because one partner was unable to fully accept the limitations and habits of the other and tried to change him/her. I anticipate the question, "What about a partner who has a problem which is hurting him? For example, what about a partner who is an alcoholic?"

Acceptance does not mean that you don't try to improve your present circumstances. It means that first you completely accept the situation you find yourself in, instead of expending valuable energy ranting, raving and bemoaning the fact that you are in that situation. You will then be able to see clearly what needs to be done, and you will have the physical, mental and emotional energy to change your present situation.

Eckhart Tolle, in his book *The Power of Now,* tells us that in every situation in which we find ourselves, we have three choices. We can change the situation we are in, or we can remove ourselves from the situation. If we cannot do any of these, for example we are in prison, the only choice we have is to accept the situation completely. Any other choice will be counter-productive and will create stress and tension in our lives. Tolle reminds us, "When you live in complete acceptance of what is, that is the end of all drama in our lives." Where there is no drama, there is no conflict and our bodies and our minds are at peace.

The Buddha reminded his followers of this over two thousand years ago when he told them, "Serenity comes when you trade expectations for acceptance."

And Marcus Aurelius, the great Roman statesman and philosopher, emphasized the importance of acceptance when he wrote, "Accept whatever comes to you woven in the pattern of your destiny, for what could more aptly fit your needs?"

Very often, events do not turn out the way we had hoped, resulting in disappointment. When this happens, it is crucial for us to remember that we do not have the total picture. Only God, or our Higher Power, has the complete picture. The common saying, "It all happened for the best," has a great deal of truth as the following anecdote illustrates.

A fisherman was drinking with his friend one afternoon in a tavern. Although he was inebriated, he remembered that he had to go fishing that night and left to go home in his van, when the police stopped him and took him to the lock-up for driving under the influence. He was extremely upset and thought of all the money he would lose by not going to the market with a boatload of fishes.

It turned out that there was a severe storm that night and he would have certainly drowned had he gone out to sea. The following morning, he thanked his lucky stars that the police had locked him up.

The recipe for total peace, then, is to totally accept

what is. It is foolish to do otherwise.

4 FORGIVENESS

Many writers have explored the topic of forgiveness. Alexander Pope, the famous English poet, wrote in his *Essay on Criticism,* "To err is human, to forgive divine."

In her book, *IF LIFE is a GAME, THESE are the RULES,* Cherie Carter-Scott wrote that non-forgiveness, which includes anger and resentment, is linked to the ego. Not forgiving someone

. . . makes you feel superior and righteous when you can look down your nose and hold a grudge toward someone who has wronged you. However, resentment consumes a lot of energy. Why waste valuable energy on prolonged anger and guilt, when you could use that energy for far greater things? When you let go of resentment, guilt, and anger, you become revitalized and create space in your soul for growth.

Do you want to be a perpetual victim by harboring anger and resentment to those who have hurt you, or do you want to be free? Free to do the things you want to do. Free to achieve your dreams without having to carry the heavy burden of non-forgiveness.

Non-forgiveness not only saps our energy and

vitality, but produces harmful chemicals in the body which can cause a variety of illnesses in the person harboring it, while not harming in the least the person at whom it is directed.

Somebody once said, "Experiencing anger and resentment is like drinking a dose of poison and expecting the other person to die."

How true!

Nelson Mandela obviously learned this lesson. When he left prison after spending twenty-seven years in jail, he said, "As I stand before the door to my freedom, I realise that if I do not leave my pain, anger and bitterness behind me, I will still be in prison."

The same can be said for all of us. If we continue to experience anger and resentment because of the harm people have done to us, we are imprisoned by the past.

We often don't know the struggles that the person who has harmed us is experiencing, and why he behaves that way. That is why Madame de Stael wrote in her book, *Corrine,* "To understand all is to forgive all."

The question is often asked, "If I forgive a person for causing me harm, am I not allowing that person to harm me again?"

Forgiveness does not mean exposing yourself to be hurt over and over again. Rather, it is a mental process that allows you not to tense up when you think of the persons who hurt you. You should certainly isolate yourself from those who have caused you harm, but mentally forgive them for the way they behaved. For example, you would not put your hand in a nest of rattlesnakes, because you know what is likely to happen. You know that it is the nature of rattlesnakes to bite when you intrude in their territory, but you do not crunch up when you think of rattlesnakes.

The term, "I forgive you, but I do not trust you," has a great deal of merit .

Many people act the way they do because they are addicted to certain behaviors. For example, a person addicted to gossiping will carry negative news about another even if he is indebted to that person. Or he will even try to destroy a person who is his benefactor. Shakespeare explored this enigmatic behavior in the character of Iago, in his tragedy *Othello*.

We often forget that the injustices of the past include not only the harm others have done us, but the harm that we have done to others and to ourselves. Just as we expect others to forgive us for the wrongs we have committed, we must learn to forgive others for the wrongs they have done to us, and to forgive ourselves for the wrongs we have done to others, and ourselves.

In the *Lord's Prayer*, we ask God to "…forgive us our trespasses, as we forgive them that trespass against us." How many of us ask for forgiveness, but are unwilling to forgive those who have hurt us?

Carter-Scott reminds us that we all have a concept of the values which we hold dear to ourselves, and when our behaviors don't align with this concept, we experience an internal dissonance. When this happens, we should acknowledge the fact that we behaved in an inappropriate manner, and learn from our behavior, instead of harshly judging and punishing ourselves.

Carter-Scott emphasizes, "Your conscience is not your enemy; it is there to remind you to stay on track and stick to your values. Just notice the feeling it is sending you, and move on."

The *Buddhist Prayer of Forgiveness*, cited below, succinctly includes most of the ideas discussed above.

If I have harmed anyone in any way, either knowingly or unknowingly, through my own confusions, I ask their forgiveness.

If anyone has harmed me in any way, either knowingly or unknowingly, through their own confusions, I forgive them.

And if there is a situation I am not yet ready to forgive, I forgive myself for that.

For all the ways that I have harmed myself, negate, doubt, belittle myself through my own confusions,

I forgive myself.

Forgiving others and yourself will set you free from the burdens of the past, make you feel at peace in the present, and enable you to forge a brighter future.

5 AN ATTITUDE OF GRATITUDE

Psychology Today, April 3, 2015, lists several benefits of gratitude. The article suggests that gratitude is easy to practise and yet it is often overlooked, notwithstanding its enormous benefits.

A number of researchers showed that grateful people are healthier than those who are not. They have lower blood pressure; they take care of themselves better; they have lower risks of depression, and they live longer. They are also less likely to experience anger, envy, resentment, frustration and regret.

Gratitude also helps people to sleep better. That is why some researchers recommend writing in a *Gratitude Journal* before going to bed. Many people thank God for all His blessings before going to sleep.

Self-esteem also improves when we practice gratitude. When we are grateful for what we have, we are less inclined to compare ourselves with others. Grateful people are happy instead of being resentful when others succeed.

Mental resilience is another benefit of gratitude. When we are grateful for what we have, we will not be discouraged by setbacks, because our focus is on our many blessings.

Deepak Chopra, a well-known self-help writer, tells us that a chemical is secreted in our bodies with every thought we entertain. When we think pleasant thoughts like gratitude, "feel good" chemicals such as endorphins are produced within our bodies. Conversely, when we think negative thoughts like envy and resentment, the production of harmful chemicals such as adrenaline prepares us for the fight or flight response.

Many people take their blessings for granted and instead of being grateful, focus on what they don't have. Yet, if they are asked the question, "Would you give up what you have for a billion dollars?" most of them will answer, "No!"

Only a very foolish person would give up their five senses for any amount of money. I recovered from a stroke some years ago, and have a few relatives and friends who have had strokes. Many of them cannot walk or talk, and I remind myself of this often when I walk across the room or talk with my family and friends. I am grateful to God for allowing me to retain these abilities.

It is easy to practise gratitude in our everyday lives. Imagine someone holding a door for you. You can just walk through without saying anything, or you can thank the person sincerely and heartily. When you say, "Thank you!" that person will be appreciative of you, and will feel better about himself or herself. So will you. It is not surprising that grateful people have more friends and enduring relationships than those who are ungrateful, or those who do not express their gratitude.

We all have the ability and opportunity to cultivate and express gratitude. Simply take a few moments when you wake up in the morning, during the day, and when you go to bed at night to focus on all that you have. Before you know it, gratitude will be an essential part of your life.

Make a commitment to develop an attitude of gratitude and to express gratitude daily. It will take nothing from you and it will make others feel better. So will you.

6 DO WE LIVE IN A FRIENDLY UNIVERSE?

Albert Einstein, the famous mathematician, said that the most important question we can ask ourselves is this: "Is the universe a friendly place?"

It appears to be an enigma that a prominent mathematician who was engaged with facts would say this, but we should accept Einstein's statement that our perceptions of the world are important because they determine how we see the world and live our lives.

Einstein recognized the fact that, unlike immutable mathematical laws, we have control over our perceptions by changing the way we regard and respond to the objective world. And our perceptions determine whether we are happy and serene, or fearful and anxious. These feelings determine our actions.

If we perceive the world as a friendly place and regard the people who live in it as friendly, we behave in a relaxed and helpful manner, and our lives will be positive and rewarding. We are also likely to achieve more because we do not expend our energies worrying and experiencing resentment and anxiety.

On the other hand, if we perceive the world as a hostile and dangerous place, we will always be fearful and apprehensive and our actions will be aggressive. We will go about our affairs in a competitive manner, view the people we meet with suspicion, and regard them as rivals in our fight for survival. Our energies will be depleted by these negative feelings and resulting actions.

Our perceptions of ourselves determine how we perceive the universe. Rachel Jamison Webster, a poet and associate professor of English, described her feelings as she was working on a project to support her partner as he was dying from ALS:

> *The universe is not friendly to a small, egocentric self. Everything we think we are, we're going to lose; death comes to all of us. But because we are the universe—we are of it and it is of us, with no real separation—it is not unfriendly. I believe in a harmony, and elegance and wholeness that is both right here with us and inside us, and also way beyond our comprehension.*

Other writers support the above philosophy. For example, Elizabeth Larsen, economics major and winner of the 2014 Circumnavigators Travel-Study Grant, wrote about her experiences when she visited seven countries, where she studied malnutrition. She was impressed by the perceptions of the people involved and noted, "I was struck by the ability of people to maintain the view that the universe is inherently friendly. So you can see the question as a self-fulfilling prophecy. The universe is only as friendly or unfriendly as we choose it to be."

Jeff Bell, author of *Make Belief*, emphasized his belief that the universe is friendly when he wrote:

> *Actually, as a guy who makes his living delivering the news, I assure you I am all too familiar with our current mix of depressing and distressing news: the terrorist attacks, migration*

crises, mass shootings, political mudslinging, tragic deaths of all kinds, etc., etc. I report on this stuff every day. I see the bad all around us. And yet, I still choose to see the universe as friendly. And if you're willing to, as well, your life will never be the same.

Bell stressed that this does not mean that we will always get what we want which may not fit into God's plans for us, because we do not have the total picture. Only God, or your Higher Power, or the Universe, or whatever term you want to use, has the bigger picture, and does what is best for you.

If you see the universe like this, how can it not be friendly?

In *Psychology Today*, Bell outlined some strategies developed by his Advocacy partner Shala Nicely to assist us in our efforts to perceive the world as friendly.

The authors say that one reason that humans have survived is that our brains are wired to look for the negative—for things that can go wrong. This might have been okay when our ancestors were fighting for survival and had to be on a constant look out for danger, but it's no longer the case. The problem is that by directing our attention to harmful things, we miss the things that are right in this world. We should notice the positive in our lives as much as, if not more than the negative.

The fact that we don't know what's good and what's bad for us is driven home powerfully in what's known as the *Chinese Farmer Parable*.

A Chinese farmer and his son lived in a small village, and one day they woke up to find their only horse had disappeared. The farmer looked at his crestfallen son, who had no horse to plow the field, shrugged his shoulders, and said, "This may be bad. This may be good. Who knows?"

The following morning, the farmer and his son looked out their window and saw their paddock filled with an entire herd of horses that had come home with the missing horse, who stood proudly in the middle of the enclosure. The farmer looked at his jubilant son, who was jumping up and down because he had 20 horses to plow the field, and he said with the same shrug, "This may be good. This may be bad. Who knows?"

The son decided to tame one of the new horses, but in the process fell off and broke his leg. The father, helping his injured son into bed, said the same old line which the son was beginning, to believe: "This may be bad. This may be good. Who knows?"

As the sun rose the next morning, the son and the farmer watched as the Chinese army came by, conscripting all the able-bodied young men into the army. The son was excused because of his broken leg. This time, the son pre-empted the father, and declared with a twinkle in his eye, "This may be good. This may be bad. Who knows?"

The above story clearly supports the philosophy that we may feel sad or happy about a particular situation, but we should avoid judgements whether it is good or bad, due to our limited perceptions.

Instead, we should reinforce our belief that we live in a friendly universe, act accordingly, and witness positive things happening in our lives.

7 YOUR PURPOSE IN LIFE (DHARMA)

The question, "Why am I here?" is often asked by many people. Hindus have a special word for your purpose in life. The word is *Dharma*, and it means that we have taken manifestation in physical form to fulfill a purpose.

Deepak Chopra, in his book *THE Seven Spiritual Laws OF SUCCESS,* explains that, "Everyone has a purpose in life. . . a unique gift or special talent to give to others." Nobody else has your unique combination of skills and talents, and your unique way of using those skills and talents.

To find your purpose in life, Chopra says that you should find a way to use your unique talents to help humanity.

Wayne Dyer compared this uniqueness to our fingerprints, and expressed the concept of using our skills and talents to serve fellow humans in his book, *Happiness is the Way.* Wayne Dyer advised his readers to "Follow Your Bliss," and wrote, "I think we all show up here with a mission. The essence of it is to discover what makes you happy, and if it causes no harm to others, then do it."

Wayne Dyer explained how he followed his bliss. He was a teacher and a counsellor, and gave up his job to write full time, because he realized that writing was what he wanted to do. He wrote the best-selling book, *Your Erroneous Zones,* and when that was a success, he went on write many other books. He was also a successful motivational speaker.

I had the same experience when I joined the army as an infantry officer. Although I was quite successful in that role, I came to the realization that my purpose in life was to serve as an educator. I left the army, returned to the field of education, and although my career was not nearly as glamorous as the one I had as an army officer, I never looked back. I reflect with great satisfaction on all the students I was able to positively influence.

To discover your purpose in life, you have to be inspired to discover your spiritual *self.* You can do this by meditation, or by deep introspection to discover the *God essence in you.* When you can do what you love doing, and what you are good at doing, work becomes a joy.

Khalil Gibran explains this concept beautifully in his book, *The Prophet*:

Work is love made visible.

And if you cannot work with love but only with distaste, it is better that you should leave your work and sit at the gate of the temple and take alms of those who work with joy.

Sometimes, we are placed is situations in which we cannot do what we love at a particular time. Most immigrants to Canada and other countries have found themselves in such situations. When you find yourself in this situation, do the job to which you were assigned to the best of your ability.

For example, I was a co-op teacher before I retired, and many of my students who were office administrators and accountants in their home countries complained that they were given tasks like filing and photocopying which were below their ability. I gave them the example of my brother, Dwarka, who worked on a pig farm when he first went to North Carolina. Although it was not the job he was trained to do, he did a great job. The owner told him, "You are no ordinary farm worker. You are doing a very good job, but there is more to you than a farm worker. Tell me about yourself."

Dwarka told him about his background—that he had graduated with a B.A. from the University of Guyana, but he had just immigrated to the United States, and had to work to support his family. The owner replied, "My wife is on the board of trustees at Brunswick Community College. I'll ask her to talk to the President and see what he can do for you."

Dwarka was hired as a part-time instructor in the Continuing Education Department of the college, and he did such a good job that after a while he was promoted as head of the department. He was subsequently hired as the president of a bible college, and is now the head of the communications department in a large community college.

All because he did a good job at a pig farm.

I reminded the students that if they could not do a good job of filing and photocopying, the co-op supervisor would not trust them to perform more challenging tasks.

I hope that you will find your *Dharma*. Meanwhile, if you are stuck in a dull job, remember the words of Mother Teresa: "Not all of us can do great things. But we can do small things with great love," and endeavor to perform your task with love and enthusiasm.

8 SELF-JUDGMENT

Most of us often judge others, but we judge ourselves even more often, and more harshly, than we judge others.

In the past, almost all of us have behaved in ways which we have regretted, and it is important that we learn from our mistakes and adjust our behavior. However, it is also crucial for us to distinguish our own behavior in particular situations from our deepest selves. We are God's creatures, and we deserve love and respect from ourselves and others.

Good parents observe this principle when they tell their children who misbehave, "I love you very much, but I do not like it when you behave this way."

Self-judgement is almost an unconscious process, because it is automatic and we are only peripherally aware of our self-talk, most of which is negative. Shad Helmstetter, in his book *WHAT TO SAY WHEN YOU TALK TO YOURSELF* wrote: "Leading behavioral researchers have told us that as much as *seventy-five* percent of everything we think is negative, counterproductive, and works against us."

The first step towards avoiding self-blame is to know we are engaged in this negative self-talk, and then stop the flow of energy to the thought, instead of feeding the voice, or in some cases the committee, in our heads.

Max Lucado, a pastor and an author wrote, "Feed

your faith, and your fears will starve to death." I take this to mean that, instead of giving energy to the negative thoughts of blaming ourselves, we should consciously change our thoughts to more positive ones.

It is difficult, if not impossible to think two thoughts at the same time. That is why affirmations are extremely useful in replacing negative thoughts with positive ones. Affirmations like the one below will remind you that you are a child of God and that you are deserving of peace and fulfillment.

"I am filled with love, peace and forgiveness of myself and others for errors of the past. I am healthy and well. I am joyful and happy."

You can develop a set of affirmations tailored to your specific needs. Remember that affirmations can be changed or modified, based on your circumstances. They should affirm you as a valuable human being, who deserves the best in life.

Whenever you find yourself opening old wounds, repeat the affirmations to replace the negative thoughts, just as you would plant flowers in your garden to choke out the weeds.

Deepak Chopra, a self-help writer, says that we often sympathize with our friends, but we do not extend the same sympathy to ourselves. It is important to be sympathetic towards yourself, just as you would be towards a friend. Remember that you are your own best friend.

Lara d'Entremont, a writer, emphasizes the importance of being kind to ourselves: "We would never tell someone he should condemn himself—that such negative self-talk is good for him. But we often do not make that argument to ourselves."

How true!

Make a commitment to be kind to yourself and while it is crucial that you learn from your mistakes, abandon all self-blame. You'll then be able to live your life free of energy-draining regrets and be at peace with yourself and the world.

9 BE IMPERFECTLY PERFECT

In his book, *Don't Sweat the Small Stuff,* Richard Carlson, has a chapter entitled, "Make Peace with Imperfection."

He stresses that the need for perfection and the desire for inner tranquility conflict with each other. If we always strive for perfection, we will never achieve inner peace, and we will never be grateful for what we have, and for what we are.

When we view our quest for perfection in this way, we can see that perfection is linked to gratitude. Striving for perfection implies that we focus on what is wrong with us, and we are always striving for more, instead of being content and grateful for what we are and what we have.

When we focus on what is wrong, we become dissatisfied and discontented with what *is*. This leads to judgement of ourselves and of other people.

Contentment with our perfectly imperfect lives is also linked to the principle of acceptance. When we completely accept the situation in which we find ourselves, our bodies and minds are more relaxed. We can then better improve our lives, because we do not waste time and energy being dissatisfied.

There was a period in my life, when I would not accept where I was at a particular time, and I always wanted to be somewhere else. In addition, I always wanted to be like somebody else whom I perceived as being perfect, rather than accept my imperfect self.

Romans 3:23 tells us, "For all have sinned and fall short of the glory of God."

This implies that we are all imperfect. Most of us are anxious and fearful because we do not accept this imperfection in ourselves, and in others.

When we do not accept imperfection in ourselves, and expect to have perfect wives, husbands, girlfriends, or boyfriends, perfect children, perfect neighbors and friends, the result is a great deal of stress.

Catch yourself when you fall into the habit of insisting that things should be other than what they are. And gently remind yourself that life is okay the way it is right now. In the absence of your judgement, everything would be fine.

As you eliminate the need for perfection in all areas of your life, you'll begin to discover the perfection of life itself. By this I mean, your inner self, your true spirit, your perfect *God being*. All the rest are external things, and some of them are sure to be imperfect.

In his very powerful book, *Secrets for Success and Inner Peace,* Dr. Wayne Dyer has an entire chapter entitled "Wisdom is Avoiding All Thoughts That Weaken You."

Some of these thoughts are shame, guilt, apathy and anger. Why do we think these thoughts which we know produce negative emotions? Because we think that we and others should behave perfectly.

Deepak Chopra reminds us constantly that every

thought produces a chemical. All the negative thoughts about imperfection cause the body to produce many chemicals that are harmful to the body.

On the other hand, if we are willing to accept our own imperfections and the imperfections of others, we will think thoughts of peace, joy, love, acceptance and willingness. And our bodies will produce chemicals that calm and heal us.

So, let's accept our imperfection, the imperfection of others, the imperfection of events and things around us, and live perfectly imperfect lives.

10 GIVING AND RECEIVING

Deepak Chopra, a prominent writer and public speaker, compares giving and receiving to the flow of blood in our bodies. He says that when the blood stops flowing, it begins to clot and coagulate.

The same is true of life. We should give and receive freely, instead of holding on to things. For example, hoarding money will stop the flow of energy.

Chopra says that all of us, however poor we may be, have the ability to give something to everybody we meet. It does not have to be money or things. A kind word, a compliment, a prayer, or a smile will be enough. Or we can give of our time and do a kind deed.

The gift of your time is even more valuable than the gift of money or other physical objects. The famous philosopher Kahlil Gibran wrote, "You give but little when you give of your possessions. It is when you give of yourself that you truly give."

For example, when my children were small, they received many presents from me, my wife, and our many relatives. They were grateful for all the presents they received, but the relatives they still think most fondly of are the ones who took the time to sit with them and play games, or put together jigsaw puzzles.

Gibran writes that we should give freely, regardless of who deserve it or not. He asks whether the trees in our orchards or our flocks ask whether we deserve to receive? He stresses that we all deserve God's grace and forgiveness.

Therefore, we should not perceive ourselves as judges of who deserve our generosity. Referring to our judgements as to who deserve our gifts, Gibran asks, "And who are you that men should rend their bosoms and unveil their pride, that you may see their worth naked and their pride unabashed?"

How should we give? When we share bread with another, we can share it as one human being to another, or we can share it as one who has plenty, and gives out of pity to those who are in need. There is a big difference. In the cases cited above, both shared bread with another, but how they gave mattered perhaps even more than the giving.

That is why many people claim that who we are is more important than what we do.

Make a commitment to give something to the people you meet, to brighten their lives and your own life. And do so with love, as one human being to another.

Along with giving, we must also learn to receive graciously. Most of us know how to give, but the art of receiving is more difficult. Chopra says that every relationship is one of give and take, and if you interrupt the flow of either, you interfere with nature's intelligence.

When you receive a gift gracefully, you are giving a gift to the giver, who is a representative of the universe, and has decided to share with you—also a representative of the universe.

I was reminded of this when I was a teacher of co-op education in a class of adult students. Students liked to give teachers small gifts at the end of each class as tokens of their appreciation. I told my students not to give me any presents, because I didn't need anything. The teacher with whom I co-taught the class, Pat Marion, scolded me. "Ken," she chastised, "the students want to show their appreciation for all the time and effort you put into preparing them for the workplace, and for finding them appropriate placements. You are telling them that you don't want anything from them. Do you think that you're too great to receive small presents from your students?"

Realizing that I was stopping the flow of giving and receiving, I relented and took the advice of Alexander McCall Smith who in his book, *Love Over Scotland*, writes, "Gracious acceptance is an art—an art which most never bother to cultivate. We think that we have to learn how to give, but we forget about accepting things, which can be much harder than giving. Accepting another person's gift is allowing that person to express his or her feelings for you."

Some people have problems accepting the gift of praise. For example, I visited the workplace of one student in my co-op class, and her supervisor told me that when she complimented the student on an accounting task she had completed, the student responded, "Oh, that's nothing. When I was in India, I was head of the accounting department, and I did much more difficult tasks than that."

The supervisor said that she felt deflated.

I realised then that in our class discussions on how to handle constructive criticism, I had neglected to discuss how to handle praise.

When somebody tells us that we are wearing a nice shirt or dress, how many of us say, "Oh, this old thing! I just picked it out of the closet," instead of saying, "Thank you! I'm glad you like it."

Perhaps the art of giving and receiving can best be summed up in *The Prayer of St. Frances of Assisi*:

Lord, make me an instrument of thy peace!

That where there is hatred, I may bring love.

Where there is wrong, I may bring the spirit of forgiveness.

Where there is discord, I may bring harmony.

What is noticeable about this quote is that St. Frances was not praying for riches to benefit himself, but prayed for the Lord to give him strength to bring peace, love, forgiveness and harmony in the world. He prayed to receive in order to give.

Make a commitment to keep the energy flowing—to practise giving and receiving gracefully, and watch magic happen in your life.

11 WHAT QUESTIONS DO YOU ASK YOURSELF?

The questions which we ask ourselves are very important because they determine our actions which lead us to success or failure. This is because our brains always work faithfully to provide answers to our questions, to confirm what it believes to be true. The brain does not distinguish between real and imagined events. For example, when athletes imagine they are practicing for a particular event, their brains fire up the exact muscles they will use when they are physically involved in that event. To give another example, if you think of the word, *lemon,* chances are that your salivary gland will begin to secrete saliva, because the brain is preparing the body to eat a lemon.

Because the brain is always working to prove us right, it is crucial that we ask ourselves questions which will provide positive outcomes, rather than negative ones.

For example, if we are faced with an obstacle, and we ask ourselves, "Why does this always happen to me?" our brains will come up with several reasons why difficulties always come our way. On the other hand, if we ask ourselves, "How can I deal with this challenge?" our brains will work overtime to find ways to deal with the situation.

If we ask ourselves a particular question such as, "Why am I so lucky?" our brains will come up with several reasons why we are lucky, and will guide us to actions that prove that things will always go our way.

Our brains will also work to prove us right if we ask ourselves, "Why am I so unlucky?" It will guide us to actions that prove that we are unlucky, and we will feel satisfied that we were right. Few feelings give us more satisfaction that being right.

One of my younger brothers. Dwarka always claimed that luck was on his side and it was not surprising that things always worked out for him. He repeatedly told me, *Buddy, I should have died many times, and yet I am still here. Over time, I have been faced with many difficulties, and my life was repeatedly threatened, but I always asked myself, How can I turn this setback into an opportunity?*

When he was living in Guyana, his life and the lives of the members of his family were in danger because of his close relationship with Dr. Walter Rodney, a political figure who was assassinated. Dwarka decided to remove himself and his family from the situation, left Guyana and fled to the Bahamas, where they spent several years before immigrating to the United States. Despite the difficulties he and his family encountered, he steadfastly believed in his own ability to prosper, and constantly asked himself, "What can I do to succeed?"

At the time of my writing this passage, he is the coordinator of the communications department in a large community college and is the president/founder of the *New Millenium Ministries*. He is also the acknowledged spiritual advisor of our extended family.

Of course, the questions we ask ourselves are related

to our self-concept. One motivational speaker, Robert Rosen reminds us:

> *Self-reflection entails asking yourself questions about your values, assessing your strengths and failures, thinking about your perceptions and interactions with others, and imagining where you want to take your life in the future.*

He advises that, without being unrealistic, be positive about your own value and ask questions that affirm your self-worth. If the questions you ask yourself are positive, you will have positive outcomes, and chances are that you will be successful in life.

Some of the questions we ask ourselves are based on the conditioning we received in our lifetimes. How many times were we told that we couldn't do something, that we didn't have the aptitude or the skills to complete a particular task? When we were given negative messages by people who had the authority and power over us, we tended to believe them, and consequently fostered negative perceptions of ourselves. Of course, these perceptions determine the questions we ask ourselves. We can overcome this negative conditioning by repeatedly affirming our self-worth.

The questions we ask ourselves are a form of self-talk. Shad Helmstetter, in his insightful book *WHAT TO SAY WHEN YOU TALK TO YOURSELF,* stresses the importance of giving ourselves positive messages. If we constantly repeat affirmations like the one given below, the questions we ask ourselves will empower us and foster positive actions leading to success:

> *I am an exceptional human being. My goals and my incredible belief in myself turn my goals into reality. I have the power to live my dreams. I believe in them like I believe in myself. And that belief is so strong that there is nothing that diminishes my undefeatable spirit.*

When we believe in ourselves, we will ask questions of ourselves that strengthen us and enable us to reap the rewards we justly deserve. So let us resolve to ask ourselves questions that empower us.

12 CONTENTMENT

Over two thousand years ago Epictetus, wrote, "Fortify yourself with contentment, for this is an impregnable fortress." His advice, which is still relevant today, is echoed by many relatively modern writers.

Samuel Johnson reminds us: "Of the blessings set before you, make your choice and be content. No man can taste the fruits of autumn while he is delighting his scent with the flowers of the spring; no man can, at the same time, fill his cup from the source and from the mouth of the Nile." Johnson thus reminds us that we should be content wherever we are, instead of wishing to be somewhere else, or sometime in the future.

Many religious texts exhort us to be content...

Psalm 118:24 tells us, "This is the day the Lord has made; we will rejoice and be glad in it." It is important to note that the emphasis is on this day, not yesterday or tomorrow.

Contentment is again stressed in 1 Timothy, 6:6-7: "But godliness with contentment is great gain. For we brought nothing into the world, and we can take nothing out of it."

The Bhagwat Gita stresses that *liberation* comes from delight in the *self*, contentment with the *self*, *self-realization* and *self-fulfillment*.

And the Quran says that having true faith and true

submission to Allah means that we will be content, and therefore happy about everything else in life, because we know it to be from Allah alone.

Many psychologists and self-help writers stress that we should treasure each moment, live in it, and be content in it. If we can learn to enjoy each moment of our lives, many personal problems will disappear. Eckhart Tolle, author of *The Power of Now,* asks, "What problems do you have at this moment?" He stresses that he is not talking about an hour from now, or even five minutes from now, but THIS MOMENT. If we live in this moment, and be grateful for it, we will be filled with contentment.

When I wake up in the morning, I am content to find myself above ground. I am content that I can breathe without any difficulty, because I know that many people experience difficulties breathing. I am content that I can get up out of bed, walk to the kitchen, and make and enjoy a cup of coffee.

Sometimes, we forget to be content with our ability to go about our everyday activities, when many people cannot. I can remember returning to school one September after the summer break, and my principal asked me, "How are you, Ken?"

"Very good, Carol. I can walk," I replied.

When she gave me a puzzled look, I knew that I owed her an explanation, and told her that I had just returned from visiting my brother-in-law in London, England. He had a stroke and couldn't walk or talk, and I was just content that I could do those things.

Sally Kempton, a teacher of yoga and meditation,

says, "Most of us know how to practice discontentment. We say, 'When such and such happens, then I'll be happy.'" Kempton asks, "Why wait for happiness when it's available to you right now, at this moment?"

She continues, "We routinely sabotage our good moods by worrying about the future, grumbling about the people in our lives, and telling ourselves negative stories."

Doctors tell us that whenever we have a thought, a chemical goes with it. If we have feelings of discontent, there is an unease in the body, which produces adrenaline to get us ready for the *fight or flight* response. However, calming thoughts like contentment, produce chemicals like serotonin, which relax the body.

How can we achieve contentment?

Contentment can be achieved by looking at life from a perspective of abundance instead of from what is lacking. Instead of yearning for what you don't have, accept and enjoy what you do have.

Does contentment mean that we must not strive to achieve and make our current situations better? Not at all! Paradoxically, contentment allows us to free our bodies and our minds, and enables us to achieve more than when we are in a state of anxiety and stress. We don't need a psychologist to tell us that we have more physical, mental and emotional energy when we are contented and relaxed.

Norman Vincent Peale devoted an entire chapter entitled, "A Peaceful Mind Generates Power," in his book, *The Power of Positive Thinking*. Peale observes that we sleep better, and have much more energy when we fill our minds with peaceful and calming thoughts.

If our minds are full of worry and anxiety, we are like a driver whose vehicle is stuck in the mud, and who keeps on revving his vehicle and spinning his wheels. His vehicle is burning fuel and wearing out parts, but is going nowhere.

I have a very close friend, who always appears calm, but has such a tremendous amount of energy that a mutual acquaintance described him as, "having the gentleness of a kitten, with the power of a lion."

When I asked my friend his secret to having so much energy he replied, "My wife and I go to sleep laughing and wake up laughing. We are happy and content with our lives."

His story demonstrates that paradoxically, to effect change in your life, practice being content with what you have. You will have more energy to pursue your goals while being content with, and enjoying the present moment.

13 ANXIETY

Most of us have felt anxious at one time or another, for example, when we are going for an interview, when we are starting a new job, or when we are scheduled to give an important presentation. However, when we feel anxious constantly without any external factors triggering the anxiety, there is a problem.

In the August 2023 edition of the *Reader's Digest,* there is an interesting article entitled, "How Feeling Anxious Can Be a Good Thing." The writer, Patricia Pearson, cites Tracey Dennis-Tiwary who recently published her book, *Future Tense: Why Anxiety Is Good for You (Even Though It Feels Bad).*

Dennis-Tiwary recounts the time when she was working on a project, and had a "cloud of free-floating anxiety." Instead of suppressing her anxiety, she leaned into it, and discovered that she had neglected one important aspect of her project. She wrote down two or three things that she could do about it, and went back to sleep. Because she took action as a result of her anxiety, she felt calmer the following morning.

Dennis-Tiwari cites the announcement by experts in the World Health Organization in March 2022 that the prevalence of anxiety and depression had increased globally by 25% over the year before. The experts thought that it should be a wake-up call to all countries to step up mental health services and support. However, Dennis-Tiwari argues that anxiety can be an adaptive strategy which helps us to prepare for an uncertain future, and to plan and imagine possible scenarios.

Dennis-Tiwari's arguments may be valid for short-term anxiety, but in her article Patricia Pearson does not address the negative effects of persistent anxiety when there are no external factors to cause it.

We cannot make lists, and we cannot speculate how we will act if a specific situation should arise. We continue to be anxious, although we are aware of the myriads of problems, including, or perhaps especially, health issues that are caused by chronic anxiety.

I have experienced this kind of angst, and coped with heart palpitations and stress when there was nothing in my physical surroundings to cause me anxiety. The result was psoriasis, which resulted in higher levels of anxiety. I experienced this anomaly for a long time, and the suffering is almost indescribable. Understanding the battle that chronic anxiety sufferers face is almost impossible unless you have experienced this particular mental condition.

One poet, Olivia Likens, comes close to revealing the agony felt by people who experience persistent anxiety when she wrote:

> *I am afraid of the shadows of my mind of the twisted and warped reality I am living in. And I scream, because it is all in my head. I scream because none of it is real.*

People in the health field are becoming increasingly aware that chronic anxiety is a debilitating illness, and doctors now prescribe a variety of medications to alleviate the symptoms. Sunnybrook Hospital in Toronto has an entire wing devoted to patients who experience chronic anxiety.

Along with medication prescribed by health professionals, physical and psychological help are available, and chronic anxiety sufferers are encouraged to avail themselves of the assistance offered. Focussing on the everlasting present through meditation and relaxation techniques will alleviate symptoms of anxiety.

Remember, the bible repeatedly exhorts us not to be anxious. During his famous Sermon on the Mount, Jesus counselled, "Therefore do not worry about tomorrow, for tomorrow will worry about itself. Each day has enough trouble of its own."

Many psychologists and self-help writers repeatedly emphasize that we must learn to live in the present moment. It is difficult to experience anxiety if we relax, focus on our breathing, and feel the energy field within our bodies. This is because it is impossible to be totally relaxed and anxious at the same time.

One writer, Sukuzi, from NYU recommends meditation and exercise to deal with anxiety. Health professionals agree that one of the best strategies to deal with nervous tension is regular and vigorous exercise.

The important thing for sufferers of chronic anxiety to know is that you are not alone, and that there is help in the form of medication and psychological and physical therapy. If you are prepared to follow the advice of your doctor or therapist, you can alleviate the anxiety symptoms.

14 DO NOT HIDE YOUR LIGHT UNDER A BUSHEL

The popular philosopher and writer, Deepak Chopra, reminds us that each of us has at least one unique ability and a unique way of expressing that ability, that nobody else in the world possesses. However, many of us do not make use of that ability to help either ourselves or our fellow human beings, because we are either too afraid of failure, too shy, or too involved in other activities. In other words, we conceal our God-given talents, rather than offer them to the world.

In Matthew 5:15-16, Jesus says, "Neither do men light a candle, and put it under a bushel, but on a candlestick; and it giveth light unto all that is in the house. Let your light so shine before all men..."

Sharing your light does not diminish your own light, just as lighting a candle from a match does not lessen the fire from the match. Instead, it brings light where there was darkness.

You can let the light within you shine in several ways. You can live your life so that it is an example to others. Most of us know at least one person who lived, or is living a life, that we admire, and is an example of how life should be lived, regardless of the religious beliefs of that person. For example, Mother Teresa lived her life in selfless service to others. She founded *Missionaries of Charity*, an organization which assisted the poor and the sick, and helped numerous people, while she asked nothing for herself. One couple who lived in my village, was childless. They unassumingly helped the people around them with their children in the form of time, gifts from their farm, and frequently money. At the time they did this, I did not recognize the value of their actions, but time and reflection have revealed the value of their selfless acts of spreading their light of kindness.

Another person in the village was an absolute wizard with his hands and could repair anything, from clocks to motor cars. Villagers called him *Mr. Fix It,* and he used his God-given talent to help others. Very often, his pay was a few drinks and a meal. Again, I did not truly value his work until recently, but I now realize the time and expense he saved so many of his fellow villagers by employing his special talent to serve them.

People can use their skills that God has given them to serve humanity and help others in a variety of ways. The November 2023 issue of the *Reader's Digest* describes the work of an engineer, Yasmeen Lari, who was involved in designing many high-rise buildings for wealthy clients in Pakistan until she decided that she would rather use her skills to help the less fortunate— many of them disaster victims. She designed buildings made from zero carbon bamboo structures covered with sand and lime, and which were able to withstand floods

.

Another way to reach out to your fellow human beings is by sharing your blessings with others. The blessings you share can be in the form of money, your time and knowledge, food for those in need, or a simple smile or encouragement to those you meet in every-day life. Make a commitment to leave the people you meet better than when you met them. I know of one quiet, unassuming teacher, who prefers not to be named, and who stayed in school frequently until the early evening to help students who needed assistance. He was acknowledged by his students and fellow teachers by being nominated for and winning the *Prime Minister's Award for Excellence in Teaching*. Many of his students have succeeded and have become doctors, engineers, and other professionals because he took the time to share his light of knowledge with them.

You can share your light by giving compliments. I remember walking around my neighborhood, and an elderly gentleman was working in his well-kept garden. I stopped and told him how much I admired his garden whenever I walked that route. His face beamed with pride, as he stood up and shared with me how much time and effort he was investing in the garden. We are good friends today, and I stop and talk with him for a few minutes whenever I pass by his home.

You can perform simple tasks which help others, even when you're not expected to. When I moved to the current home, I wondered what type of neighbors I'd have. Of course, they were also wondering what type of people were moving in. There is no fence dividing my neighbor's front yard from mine, and whenever I cut the grass on my front yard, I simply took a few more minutes and cut the grass on his. He reciprocated, and now, in an unspoken agreement, whoever cuts his front lawn, cuts both.

Sharing your light does not mean that you must do great things. We all cannot do great things, but little acts of kindness add up and they do not require a great deal of time, effort, or money.

So, do not hide your light under a bushel, but let it shine and make your corner of the   world a brighter place.

15 INTENT VERSUS IMPACT

The term *Intent vs. Impact* is used because it is possible for someone to do or say something which causes harm to others, without intending to do so. Anti-discrimination activists caution us to be alert to this type of behavior. For example, if we imitate somebody's accent in an attempt at humor, it is reasonable to assume that the person whose accent is imitated will be hurt.

This is true even when the person affected is in a position of power. I was a teacher in a high school in an upper-middle class neighborhood, and some of my students made fun of my Guyanese accent. I informed them that I wrote my Ph.D. thesis on *An Analysis of Reading Instruction of West Indian Creole Speaking Students,* and reminded them that as a teacher, I was supposed to have a certain amount of power in the classroom. Despite this, I expressed how I felt humiliated by their imitation of my accent, and told them that I could only imagine how students who spoke the Creole dialect, and who had much less power than I did, felt when they were made fun of because of their accents.

Many people explain hurtful behavior by stating there was no intent to harm anyone. Human rights advocates respond to this by claiming that the person ought reasonably to have known that his/her action would cause harm. Making fun of someone's culture reveals negative attitudes towards that culture, because if someone respects a culture, he/she will not make fun of it.

People may also unconsciously behave in a manner that reveals their belief that one race is superior to other races. For example, I was the Antiracist Consultant in a Board of Education, and a Black male teacher, a White female teacher and I were developing antiracist materials for students in the junior high schools. Our supervisory officer came to the room in which we were working and asked me, "Ken, are you pushing them?"

I was on the verge of responding that they didn't need pushing when the white female teacher exclaimed, "I am pushing them."

Apparently, she felt that as a White person, it was her role to push people who were not White. Without realising it, she was imposing a heavy psychological burden on herself simply because she was White. The Black teacher and I discussed the situation afterwards and we expressed how diminished we felt, because both of us were quite knowledgeable about and committed to antiracism, and were insulted that another person thought that she was "pushing us."

When I explained the impact of her behavior to the White teacher, her argument was that she wanted to demonstrate her commitment to antiracism. There was a clear dissonance between the intent of her behavior, and the impact on myself and the other teacher.

Intent vs. Impact also has significance in other areas on our lives. For example a close friend, who was born in Canada, was asked frequently where he was from because he was Black. Although the people who asked him that question probably just wanted to be friends, he felt that he would always be regarded as an immigrant because of his skin color. Contrast this with a White person who had emigrated from England five years earlier. Many people would assume that he was born in Canada.

At work, if a male worker comments frequently about how well-dressed and beautiful a female worker is, his intentions may be simply to compliment the other worker, but the female worker may feel harassed. In this instance, there is a clear difference between the intent and the impact.

If a situation arises in which your intent is good, but the impact is negative, it is crucial to listen to the person impacted as she explains why she found your actions or words hurtful or disconcerting. Do not attempt to justify your actions by saying "Yes, but…" Instead, learn from the person who has been impacted, apologise, and resolve not to repeat the behavior.

The secret is to love your fellow human beings, treasure differences in cultures, and endeavour to help others in any way you can. Human beings come in different colors, have different hair textures, and practice different cultures shaped by their environments. However, all human beings have the same needs: food, shelter, clothing, and the need to be loved.

The phrase, "Think before you speak" has a great deal of truth. Regardless of what your intent may be, before you say something to or about someone, it is a good idea to ask yourself, "Is it true? Is it kind? Will it cause harm to anyone?"

16 BALANCE

Balance is very important in our physical, mental and emotional lives, and we should strive to achieve it.

One person compared balance to tuning a piano. "When you tune a piano," he asked the tuner, "do you tune the wires tightly or loosely?"

"I cannot tune the wires too tightly," the tuner replied. "If I tune them too tightly, they will break. And I cannot tune them too loosely, or else the music will not sound clearly. I have to tune them just right—not too tightly, nor too loosely—for the music to be loud and clear."

The same is true of us. We must achieve a correct balance in every aspect of our lives for our music to be heard clearly.

One obvious area in which most of us strive to achieve and maintain balance is how we spend our time and energy between our work and our families. Some people spend too much time at work and neglect their families, while some focus on their families, and don't do justice to their work.

We should not short-change work because it is important, but the family is the bedrock of society, and we should do everything in our power to provide for and protect our families. However much we love our work, we should never be so invested in our jobs that we neglect our families.

To illustrate the hazards of spending too much time at work and neglecting your family, in an episode of *Walker,* which is an adaptation of *Walker, Texas Ranger,* the protagonist was very dedicated to his job as a Texas Ranger, and worked tirelessly to catch the bad guys and right whatever wrongs in society that he could. However, in doing so, he neglected his daughter, who got into a great deal of trouble to get his attention.

For many of us, our identities are linked to our work. For example, I retired from my job many years ago, and still find myself telling people in formal contexts, "I am a retired education officer." My identity is still linked to the job I had. But I am not my job.

One passage in *Chicken Soup for the Soul, Think Positive,* is entitled, "Finding the Real Me." The article describes a woman who was laid off from her job, with which her identity was closely linked. At first, she was devastated, but then she started cooking with her children and enjoying family meals together. Before she was laid off, she was so busy that she would just pull something out of the freezer, and warm it for dinner. After she lost her job, she found herself spending more time with her children and concluded, "It was only the beginning of discovering the real me."

Is your identity so closely linked to your job, that you cannot discover the real you?

Another article, published in the October 2021 edition of the *Reader's Digest,* and entitled *Is Work Shortening Your Life?* caught my eye. The article describes the situation in which more people worked from home during the COVID pandemic. They experienced difficulties drawing the line between work, family, and their personal lives.

The article cites a report by the World Health Organization, which "cautions that regularly working more than 55 hours a week is associated with a 35% higher risk of stroke, and a 17% higher risk of dying from heart problems caused by narrowed or blocked arteries. Working long hours does more than raise your stress level; it makes it harder to live a healthy life-style—sufficient sleep, plenty of exercise, and a balanced diet."

Many of us miss important moments in the lives of our children because we are too engrossed in our work. Children grow up so fast, that if you don't give them the time and attention to show them that you love and care for them now, it may be too late. In *Jurassic Park,* Dr. Alan Grant wanted the dinosaur that was being hatched to see him as the first object it would behold when it was hatched from the egg, so that it could be attached to him. The case of children is not as dramatic, but more important.

To illustrate the above point, when my wife and I immigrated to Canada from Guyana, I was thirty-three years old. Our two Guyanese-born daughters joined us shortly after our arrival and our son was born in Canada. My wife stayed at home to look after our three children while I worked at a full-time job, a part-time job, and went to university part-time. I wanted to get a Canadian degree and stay in the education loop, because I was looking for a job in the teaching profession.

Regrettably, I did not spend enough time with my children to bond with them. Now, they are all adults, and intellectually understand why I made the choices that I did. I endeavor to spend as much time as possible with them, but the opportunity for emotional bonding was irretrievably missed. My redemption is that I spend a great deal of time with my grand-children.

Regarding focusing solely on the job and neglecting your family, one person said, "I never met a person who said on his death-bed, that he wished that he spent more time at work, but I've heard many people say that they wished that they had spent more time with their families."

When you are dead, your job will probably be advertised before or shortly after your funeral, but it will be your family who will be there for you when you are old and need love, care and attention.

Hopefully, this realization will prompt you to strive to balance your commitment to your work and to your family.

I think that very few of us will achieve perfect balance in our work and family lives, but this should not prevent us from striving to achieve it. We should remind ourselves that we should aim for progress, not perfection.

We also need to try to achieve balance with regards to the essential ingredients in our lives. In order for us to live and be healthy, our bodies need air, water, food, sleep and exercise. Yet, if we have too much of any one of these, we create an imbalance in our bodies, which can lead to serious illnesses or death.

For example, if we breathe in too much oxygen, we suffer from what is called oxygen toxicity. This is damage of the lungs that happens from breathing in too much extra (supplemental) oxygen. It's also called oxygen poisoning and can cause coughing, trouble breathing, and in severe cases, death.

We are advised to drink about two litres of water a day, to keep the body well hydrated. However, we can die if we drink too much water.

Food is important to give us energy and nourishment. But what happens if we eat too much? Our bodies become bloated and overweight, and we find that we cannot move as nimbly as we would like to. We will also be vulnerable to diseases associated with over-eating.

The same goes for exercise and sleep. Our bodies benefit from the right amounts of these, but we will experience adverse effects if we overdo either.

What about balance in the more subtle factors in our lives?

Our greatest strengths can become weaknesses if we do not achieve the correct balance. For example, when I was interviewed for a job as a teacher, I was asked what I considered my greatest strength. My answer was that my greatest strength was my sensitivity to the needs of others. Then I was asked what I thought was my greatest weakness. I responded that I was so sensitive to the needs of students that sometimes I would go overboard, and students would take advantage of my sensitivity. I then clarified that, while being willing to accommodate students, I was resolved to work within the rules and regulations of the school. I explained that, while I was sensitive to the needs of students, I realised that my greatest strength would become a weakness if I did not try to achieve an appropriate balance.

One teacher with whom I worked, was super organised and would become upset when things were not done her way. Her greatest strength—her ability to organize—thus became her weakness.

In literature, some of our most memorable characters are people who could not achieve balance. A certain amount of ambition is good in our lives, but Shakespeare's Macbeth could not balance his ambition with a concern for the well-being of others. This created a chain of events which resulted in the murder of his king and other people whom he perceived as obstacles to the achievement of his ambition, and ultimately lead to his own demise.

Another example is that we need a certain degree of confidence to go about our daily lives, but when we do not balance confidence with self-reflection, we become arrogant and egotistic. This was King Lear's tragic flaw, which resulted in his estrangement and murder of the daughter who genuinely cared for him, and to his downfall.

The secret to be successful, peaceful and happy is to achieve balance in our lives. Although we may never achieve the perfect balance, we should always strive to reach it.

17 THE THINGS I DID NOT DO

Many people regret some of the things that they have done, but perhaps the greatest regrets of many people, including myself, are the things that they haven't done. On reflection, I realise that I did not do the things I should have done because it cost me little or no effort to do nothing. All I had to do was to ignore what was happening in front of me. In addition, I did not have the courage to take the necessary action, or to say what I should have said.

However, the sin of omission is sometimes greater than the sin of commission.

James 4:17 tells us, "So whoever knows the right thing to do and fails to do it, for him it is sin."

The 18th century Irish philosopher and politician, Edmund Burke, reminded us of the disasters which can result because of inaction: "The only thing necessary for the triumph of evil over good is for good men to do nothing."

To realize the truth of this statement, we have only to reflect on the Holocaust, when so many people and governments postponed doing anything. This inaction resulted in the deaths of over six million Jews.

Other examples of indifference include the slaughter of innocent civilians in Rwanda and Cambodia and the Rape of Nanking.

But are we really doing nothing when we take no

action? Or is our inaction an action in itself? I was the anti-racist consultant at a Board of Education and gave many workshops on *How to Handle Racial Incidents*. One thing I stressed was that when a staff member witnessed a racial incident—bullying, name calling, or physical assault—he or she was required to take some type of action. To do nothing was to condone the incident.

As far as regrets and disappointments are concerned, Mark Twain reminded us, "Twenty years from now, you will be more disappointed by the things you did not do than by the ones you did."

This is true in many areas of our lives.

How often did we intend to visit elderly or ailing relative, but procrastinated? How often did we intend to tell someone how much we appreciated the sacrifices that they made for us, but refrained from doing so? Intention is useless unless it is followed by some kind of action.

Remember the words of Samuel Johnson, who reminded us that "Hell is paved with good intentions."

The time and effort we spend in doing the correct thing can save us an enormous amount of guilt for the remainder of our lives. For example, my mother could read and write Hindi fluently but not English, and made numerous sacrifices to ensure that each of her nine children received the education they needed to enable them to live successful lives. I always intended to tell her how much I appreciated everything she did for me and my siblings, but continued to put it off. In my defense, I must mention that I come from a society that does not encourage the expression of one's feelings.

One day, during my break at the school in which I was teaching, I received a call from my father who told me that Ma was taken to the hospital because of an acute asthma attack. I left school, after telling my department head that I would be back to teach the next period. I took my father to the hospital, where we were told that my mother had passed away. I regret to this day that I never told her how much I loved her and how much I am grateful for everything that she did for us.

To give another example, I still remember when I was teaching English Language and Literature in a class of students preparing to write the *General Certificate of Education* (GCE) Examination at the Indian Education Trust College in Georgetown. One student consistently received marks in the nineties in all her subjects. However, when the results of the GCE exam came in, she failed all six subjects that she wrote.

I was astonished, and asked her whether she had written her exam number in all her answer sheets. (Students were assigned numbers instead of their names on their answer sheets.) She emphasized that she had.

She returned to school the following term for a few days and then dropped out. I wanted to ask the Deputy Head Teacher to request a review of her results, but to my eternal regret, I got caught up in my work and family life, and took no action.

In the Guyanese society at that time, the GCE exam was crucial and determined the career path of a person. I frequently wonder how the life of that student turned out and regret that I did not take any action on my intent to get the authorities to review her results.

Taking action requires courage, time and energy, but the rewards are well worth the effort. Determine to expend the time and energy required to do things that will make our world a better place, instead of looking the other way.

Let us follow the example of the Good Samaritan, who acted and ministered to the person who was injured instead of ignoring him and doing nothing.

If something needs to be done, do not commit the sin of inaction, but summon the courage and the energy to do it, so that you will not have to regret the things you did not do.

18 RESPECT

People live in communities and develop certain conventions. An important one is respect for others: our parents, the elderly, other human beings, and for the earth on which we live. For example, most of us can remember our parents' exhortations to show respect to our grandparents, our elders, and our relatives.

People demonstrate this respect in different ways, depending on the culture in which they live. In Japan, for example, respect is demonstrated by bowing. The lower you bow, the greater the respect.

In India, respect is shown by clasping the hands together, and saying the word, "Namaste," which means "I respect the divinity in you."

In many cultures, respect is based primarily on age and social status, but it is important to respect every human being and all life forms on our planet, including our planet itself. Respect is the act of valuing and honoring others as individuals; it involves treating others with dignity, kindness, and love, regardless of their gender, social status, age, or background.

Respect is based on the principle that we all have the divine within us; we all have the same basic human needs and we are all subject to death. When somebody tells you that you have nothing in common, that person should be reminded that you share one trait. In five years, or fifty years—at some point in the future—you will both become piles of dust or ashes, whether you are a CEO or the janitor of a company. This is why Norman Vincent Peale, the author of *The Power of Positive Thinking,* suggests that we all make it a habit to spend some time in a cemetery, read the epitaphs on the gravestones and remind ourselves that we will end up there.

We are reminded of our interconnectedness to other humans by John Donne in his beautiful poem, *For Whom the Bells Toll.*

No man is an island,
Entire of itself.
Each is a piece of the continent,
A part of the main.
If a clod be washed away by the sea,
Europe is the less.
As well as if a promontory were.
As well as if a manor of thine own
Or of thine friend's were.
Each man's death diminishes me,
For I am involved in mankind.
Therefore, send not to know
For whom the bell tolls,
It tolls for thee.

Many of us show respect to others, but must be reminded to respect ourselves. The words of Confucius are crucial to remember in this regard. "Respect yourself, and others will respect you."

Respecting yourself has enormous benefits. In addition to others respecting you, you are more likely to respect others.

I remember on one occasion a teacher invited me and my family to her home for dinner. Before dinner, we sat in her living room and chatted, and she took that opportunity to make some remarks which belittled me in the presence of my family.

I immediately told my wife and children, "Okay guys! It's *Red Lobster*[2] time."

As I was putting on my shoes, I rebuked her mildly. "You are very good, Lorraine. You will go a far way. But you don't have to put people down in front of their families to prove how strong you are."

On the Monday morning following this incident, she approached me and apologized profusely. "I am having a hard time at work, and I am emotionally shaky," she confided.

I told her that I forgave her, and I did forgive her. However, I explained that with all my faults, my children looked up to me as their hero, and she attempted to destroy their image of me. We parted on good terms, after she promised to be aware of her feelings and how they impacted on her respect for others.

On reflection, when I think of the times I put people down, or made fun of them, I realise that I did not fully respect myself at that time. Disrespecting others was a way of giving my ego a boost.

In addition to showing respect to ourselves and each other, it is crucial that we respect the Planet Earth which sustains us and other life forms on it. Our very survival

---

[2] Red Lobster is a well-known restaurant in Canada.

depends on this.

We can assist in the preservation of the earth by cutting down on waste and pesticides, reducing the use of plastic, planting more trees, and stop poisoning our lakes and rivers.

Respect is crucial for our survival in the societies in which we live. Let us make our world a more beautiful place by showing more respect for ourselves, for each other and for the beautiful planet that sustains us.

19 CELEBRATING AND REJOICING

Celebration has many benefits in our lives. It gives us perspective, and is a great equalizer. When we celebrate with others, we can laugh at ourselves and free ourselves from our own importance. It is difficult to take ourselves seriously when we celebrate, because celebration adds gaiety, festivity and hilarity to our lives.

Another benefit of celebration is that when we celebrate, we make other people happy, because happiness is contagious and when we have an aura of happiness, people like to be around us.

When we celebrate and dwell on the good and excellent things in life, we will be so full of good thoughts that they will tend to overshadow our problems and enable us to see them as opportunities. When we do not worry about things that can go wrong, we are likely to achieve more.

Celebration brings joy into our lives. The anticipation of joy makes us strong and able to pursue our goals despite hardships. For example, people who are learning to play the piano go through the difficult beginning stages, because they know that they will experience the joy of playing the piano when they have mastered the fundamentals.

There are many ways in which we can celebrate.

We can fill our lives with love and compassion, and have a spirit of service to other human beings, so that we can experience joy not only in our own successes, but in the successes of others. When we do this, we will be able to celebrate on a constant basis.

In order to celebrate and rejoice, we need to free our minds from anxiety or worry. Matthew 6:25 tells us, "Do not be anxious about your life, what you eat or what you shall drink, nor about your body, what you shall put on."

We can also celebrate though laughing. The *Reader's Digest* magazine has a section, "Laughter is the Best Medicine," and many medical practitioners and psychologists have confirmed the benefits of laughter. The chemistry of our bodies changes when we laugh. All our muscles relax, and our bodies produce chemicals like serotonin which produces a feeling of calm.

We can celebrate through giving. Let us remember that we can give not only gifts of boxes wrapped in beautiful paper, but we can give of our time. We can give compliments. We can give prayers to those who are experiencing difficult times. We can give to people who live far away from us, who do not have as much as we do, and who struggle to survive daily.

Given the many benefits of celebration and the various ways of celebrating, it is surprising that more people do not celebrate the many successes in life that go unnoticed. Let us make a commitment to recognize the good things that are happening in our lives and in the lives of others that give us reasons to rejoice and celebrate.

20 PROCRASTINATION

It's safe to say that at one time or another, most of us have postponed performing certain tasks until the looming deadlines forced us to complete them. However, when procrastination becomes a problem, we should try to understand why we postpone doing things, and develop some strategies that enable us to complete tasks in a timely manner.

There are many reasons why people procrastinate. Some people are perfectionists and will not start a task until they feel certain that they can do it perfectly. Such people need to develop the confidence to start the task with the realization that few of us can do a job perfectly and that mistakes are a part of learning.

Linked to the concept of perfectionism, some people procrastinate because they think of all the things that can go wrong when they start working on a task. If we continue to act on this trend of thought, many of us will not get out of bed in the mornings, because so many things can go awry. Taking action means taking risks, but the rewards are great.

Then there are the dreamers and planners. Unfortunately, all their plans remain in their heads, because they postpone taking any action to actualize them. Very often, the visions of the dreamers and planners are so unrealistic that it is almost impossible for them to take any action. I know that I belong to this group. Sometimes, it's okay to dream and plan, providing that we recognize that they are only dreams and plans. However, if we plan to act on them, it is crucial to keep them realistic.

Some people procrastinate because they commit to too many tasks. Frequently these people find it difficult to say "No" to persistent requests from friends and relatives. They need to realise that it's okay to tell others that you're too busy to commit to any new tasks.

Most of us also procrastinate because we seek immediate gratification, and engage in tasks which make us feel good. We tend to put off tasks which require some effort until we absolutely must do them, and then do not complete them to the best of our ability. We should try to remember the good feeling we experience when we face the difficult tasks head on.

The writer, F. M Fradenburgh, outlined the disadvantages of procrastination very succinctly in her poem, *Advice for Going Forward*: "Delay wastes time, weakens the will, dissipates energy, discourages ambition, and prophesies failure. Resolve, and do! Do it now!"

We needlessly waste time when we procrastinate. The saying, "Procrastination is the thief of time," is attributed to Edward Young, an English poet. Dickens made the saying popular in his novel, *David Copperfield,* when Mr. Micawber told David Copperfield, "My advice is, never do tomorrow what you can do today. Procrastination is the thief of time. Collar him."

Procrastination also takes a great mental and emotional toll on the body. Although we may tell ourselves that putting off tasks do not bother us, at some level there must be a nagging feeling that we are putting off a task that needs to be done. This creates unease in our bodies, even though this uncomfortable feeling may be borderline conscious. Doctors tell us that a chemical is produced by every thought. The chemicals produced by the feeling of unease is not beneficial. Contrast the feeling of having to do something and putting it off, with the feeling of satisfaction after successfully completing a job. The pride and the high we feel after we have done a job well is due to the flow of endorphins—feel-good chemicals. We will also have more energy if we do not procrastinate. The thought that there is something we should do, but that we are not doing it, eats away at our energy, and we feel tired without knowing the reason. Starting and completing the task free our minds, leaving us to spend our energy in more useful activities.

How do we stop procrastinating?

Most often, the most difficult thing is to start a task. Aristotle's words, "Well begun is half done," has a great deal of truth.

Making lists of tasks and placing timelines when they have to be done is an excellent way of prioritizing jobs, so that you can give attention to the most urgent ones first. Be sure that the items on the list are realistic. For example, "Going to the moon," takes up one line in your *To Do* list, but is it realistic in your situation?

Many people find that dividing the task in manageable steps and taking one step at a time is an excellent way to stop procrastinating. The good feeling that we get when we complete each step will motivate us to keep going.

If you don't always succeed because of your tendency to procrastinate, it is important to remember that you're only human. Forgive yourself and keep on trying.

It may require some effort to perform tasks which require a great deal of effort and energy, but when you see how much more you can accomplish, and how relaxed and energetic you feel when you complete tasks in a timely manner, procrastination will be something you would seek to overcome.

So stop procrastinating NOW!

21 SELF-TALK

If somebody were to conduct a survey asking people to name the person to whom they talk the most, many people are likely to name their spouses, their children, or someone close to them. But although we may not be aware of it, the person to whom we talk the most is ourselves. Unfortunately, quite a bit of this self-talk is negative.

I know that this is true for me. I live a fairly comfortable life, and have some modest accomplishments. There were many positive incidents in my life's journey, including my interactions with several remarkable persons. However, like many people, there are also some things I would have done differently.

Why then, do I focus on the negative incidents of my life, instead of the positive ones? Sometimes I wonder whether it is a survival instinct. Were our ancestors forced to remember mistakes they made that could have led to their deaths, instead of focusing on successful hunts? We no longer live in a society in which we are in immediate danger (for most of the time anyway); nevertheless, many people dwell on past mistakes.

In his revealing book, *What To Say When You Talk To Yourself,* Shad Helmstetter emphasizes, ". . . your success or failure in anything, large or small, will depend on your programming—what you accept from others, and what you say when you talk to yourself." Helmstetter goes on to explain that the brain believes the messages you send to it, and will create events in your life to make what you tell it a reality.

For example, I had a brother who unfortunately has passed away. He always called himself, "The Born Loser." Events would unfold in his favor up to a certain point, but then he would do something to sabotage himself, and everything would fall apart.

Contrast this with another brother, who has an unwavering faith in himself. Things did not always work out for him, but he had enough confidence to turn life's challenges into opportunities. For example, he was a friend of Dr. Walter Rodney during the Burnham dictatorship. Dr. Rodney was assassinated, and my brother learned that he was a target. Did he throw his hands up in surrender?

Instead of crumbling, he boarded a plane for the Bahamas, taught high school there for a while, and then immigrated to the United States. As a new immigrant, he faced many difficulties but he always told himself that he would succeed. He eventually earned a Ph.D., and is now head of communications in a large community college because he gave himself the right self-talk.

With regards to Helmstetter's comment on the relationship between our success and this programming, when we were young and relied on others for our survival, we had to accept what we were told and what we could do or not do. As we grew older, what we told ourselves was increasingly influenced by the bombardment of consumer-oriented advertisements designed to influence us in every facet of our lives.

However, we should be aware that we have a choice

to believe or reject what we hear and see on social media or elsewhere. Instead of unquestioningly accepting the messages to which we are constantly exposed, we must be careful of what we tell ourselves as a result of these messages.

We have to also be critical of what our friends and acquaintances tell us? Do they tell us that we're looking good, or do they tell us negative things about ourselves? If they focus on the negative aspects, e.g. how bad we look, how do we respond?

My mother frequently told me, "Don't let anybody *tutkay*[3] you, without saying anything."

Ma's advice was to immediately refute the observations of the speaker, and to tell yourself affirming words. I am only now beginning to realize the deep psychological implications of her advice.

Without understanding the ramifications of somebody *tutkaying* me, whenever somebody observed that I did not look so well, I simply replied, "I feel fine. You don't worry about me." In this simple exchange, I refused to internalise what the other person said, and instead told myself that I was okay. My reply suggested that the speaker look at himself and take the log out of his own eye before taking the dust out of mine.

One of my brothers would spend hours in front of the mirror searching for evidence to confirm what he was told whenever an acquaintance told him, that he didn't look so well. Of course he found numerous lines on his face which validated what he had heard. Had he told

---

[3] Tell you something bad about yourself

himself that he looked great and then looked for evidence to confirm that belief, he would have found many.

One example of when I gave myself the correct self-talk was when I was about to immigrate to Canada from Guyana. The academic registrar of the University of Guyana at that time, a very kind and helpful man, asked me, "What are you going to do in Canada?"

"I am going to work during the day, and go to university in the evenings."

"It's very cold in Canada during the winter, and most people don't want to leave their homes and go to classes after they have come home," he cautioned.

I respected and admired the academic registrar very much and could have easily internalised his advice and told myself that he was right, and that I would be too cold and tired to attend university after work. But I immediately told myself that if most people found it too cold to attend evening classes, I would be one of the exceptions because I knew what I wanted, and I knew that I was prepared to make all kinds of sacrifices to achieve my goals.

He must have thought me extremely egotistic when I replied, "You're talking about most people. You're not talking about me."

It is useful to develop self-talk for every-day life and for specific situations, for example, when you are going to give a presentation to a large group. Your self-talk should be in the present tense. When you say, "I am…" the brain registers whatever you tell yourself as true. For example, if a person who regards himself as shy tells himself frequently, "I am self-confident, and I have the ability to handle any situation," the brain is so wonderful that it will ensure that your behavior conforms to what you frequently tell it. It may take some time, but it will happen. People who know me at the time I am writing this passage may not believe that I am basically a shy person, but I keep telling myself that I act confidently in social and academic situations and it has become my reality.

You should also structure your self-talk to say what you want, not what you don't want. For example, if you wish to be able to speak confidently in front of large groups, your self-talk should be, "I feel comfortable speaking to large groups," instead of, "I am not nervous when speaking to a large group of people." In short, focus on what you want, not on what you don't want. I will discuss this concept more fully in another meditation.

A popular term for this kind of self-talk is "Affirmations." Some psychologists believe that affirmations are more powerful than meditations.

To encourage positive self-talk, make it a choice to associate with people who dwell on the positive aspects of life, instead of the negative. However, it is crucial to remember that you are the best friend you'll ever have. Be sure to give yourself positive messages when you talk to yourself.

22 OUR FEELINGS

Our feelings, not wealth or possessions, are the primary determinants of our experience in life. Most of us know poor people who go about their lives happy and contented because they feel so good about themselves. On the other hand, most of us also know people who are wealthy, but are so dissatisfied with their lives that they feel unhappy and unfulfilled.

Our feelings are the lens through which we view the world and the people in it. For example, when somebody is deeply in love, he sees the object of his love as perfect. Some years later, should he be involved in bitter divorce proceedings, the same person who was perceived as perfect will be most likely seen as evil, dishonest or manipulative. That person may not have changed greatly, but the feelings of the perceiver would have influenced his perceptions.

Richard Carlson in his book, *Don't Sweat the Small Stuff,* calls feelings "a foolproof guidance system to navigate you through life."

Our feelings let us know whether we are on track and headed towards serenity and peace of mind, or whether we are off track, and headed towards unhappiness and conflict. Basically, it lets us know what our internal weather is like.

Our feelings will always tell us what we are thinking. If we are thinking positive thoughts, our bodies will feel relaxed and peaceful. If, on the other hand, we are thinking negative, destructive thoughts, our bodies will feel tense.

The good news is that we can choose how we feel. The arguments go like this: We can choose what we think. Our thoughts determine how we feel. Therefore, we can choose how we feel.

Let's try a short exercise. Try and be angry without having an angry thought. Now try feeling stressed without first having a stressful thought. Could you do it? It's impossible! We cannot have a feeling without a thought. Unhappiness cannot exist on its own, but is the feeling that accompanies negative thinking about our lives. And there is nothing to feed that feeling, except our thinking.

How do our feelings affect our minds and our bodies? When we feel calm and relaxed our bodies produce substances like endorphins, which calm our minds and bodies. On the other hand, when we are feeling angry, resentful, depressed, stressed out and frustrated, our warning system kicks in. Our bodies get in the *fight or flight* mode and produce adrenaline, causing our entire system to be on high alert. But there is no external danger and nothing to fight, so the body starts to fight with itself. This inner conflict is the cause of many ailments, including auto-immune diseases.

When feelings of distress kick in, we need to make immediate adjustments. Carlson says that we need to act on our feelings in the same way that we respond to the warning lights on the dashboard of our vehicles. When one of the lights starts flashing, most of us check our vehicles, or take them to the garage to find out what's wrong and fix the problems. On the other hand, how many of us take some sort of action in response to our negative feelings?

Whenever we feel stressed about minor incidents in our lives, we should remind ourselves that whatever is making us stressed is small stuff in the larger scheme of things. In ten years from now, will it matter? Instead of making small incidents into emergencies, look at them from a broader perspective.

Our perception of the world also influences our feelings. Do we regard the world as basically a friendly place and view incidents as what Richard Carlson terms "one more passing show?" Or do we see life as a series of emergencies?

It is important to remember that all things that give us pleasure or pain, come and go. Pleasure and pain, approval and disapproval, achievements and mistakes, fame and shame are short-lived. Eventually, everything disappears into nothingness. Welcoming this truth into our lives is very liberating and will make us feel better.

When something is happening that we enjoy, we must accept that it will be eventually replaced by something else. And when we feel pain we should tell ourselves, "This too shall pass."

This awareness will allow us to be at one with the universe, feel a sense of serenity and be relaxed and at peace, regardless of our physical environment.

It is important that you monitor your feelings, then. They will give you a clear indication whether your life is progressing along the right path or whether you should make adjustments.

23 CHOICE

The topic of "Choice" has been debated by many philosophers. Some think that our lives are pre-ordained and we are mere pawns in the larger scheme of things, while others, like the existentialist philosopher, Kierkegaard, believed that life is a series of choices we make for ourselves.

One self-help writer, Cherie Carter-Scott, author of *IF LIFE is a GAME, THESE are the RULES*, distinguishes a choice from a decision by pointing out that a decision is made in the mind, but a choice is made in the gut.

Carter-Scott wrote, "Choice is the exploration of desire and then the selection of action. In every moment, you are choosing either to align yourself with your own true path or to veer away from it. There are no neutral actions." I totally agree with Carter-Scott because most of us have visions of what we want to achieve, or be in life. Everything we choose to do, or not to do, will either lead us towards our goals or divert us from them.

The prominent Austrian philosopher, Victor Frank, wrote, "Between stimulus and response there is a space. In that space is our power to choose our response. In our response lies our growth and our freedom."

Some of us are steadfast in making choices that conform to the perceptions we have of ourselves, while the actions of others deviate from these images. When our choices do not conform to our self-conceptions, we experience an internal dissonance which results in discomfort.

We make numerous choices throughout the day, and millions over the course of our lives; the way our lives unfold is the result of many of these choices. Some choices may have a minimal impact. For example, the choice to sleep five minutes longer in the morning is not likely to greatly influence the way our future unfolds. On the other hand, the choice whether to leave the job we've had for some time, may have momentous consequences.

On the spiritual level, the quality of our lives depends on whether we choose to believe in God or in a Higher Power. If we choose to believe in a power greater than ourselves, our choices, and our actions based on these choices on a day-to-day basis, will hinge on the belief that we are a valuable part of the universe which we are sharing with God's creatures. On the other hand, the choice to believe that we are the center of the universe will also influence our actions, our lives and our relationships with others. As a result, our actions will be self-serving.

On an environmental level, we can make choices that would preserve the beautiful earth on which we live, or act on choices that would eventually destroy it. Our choices will determine whether we live our lives in such a manner that we leave minimal footprints, or whether we focus on consumerism and leave huge carbon footprints. I constantly remind myself that each little action I take to preserve the earth will make a difference.

On a personal level, do we see other people as sharing the planet with us, or do we see them as competing for the good things in life? Our choices will determine whether we see ourselves living in a cooperative world where we perceive others as fellow human beings deserving of the blessings which our world has to offer, or whether we see them as hostile competitors for the limited resources in a competitive world.

We can also choose to be happy or unhappy, regardless of how much or how little we have. I know that this sounds far-fetched, but we can choose to do things and think thoughts that make us happy. In their best-selling book, *How to Be Your Own Best Friend*, Mildred Newman and Bernard Berkowitz tell us: "People are choosing all the time, but they don't want to admit it. You are free when you accept the responsibility for your choices. And when you choose your own best interests. It's not as hard to do as it sounds." The concepts outlined in this book will be discussed more fully in another meditation.

It is quite easy to make the right choices if we pause for a while, and ask ourselves, "Is this the right thing to do? Will it cause any harm to another human being or living thing? Will my inaction cause any harm?"

If your choice aligns with your innermost desires and does not harm anyone or any of God's creations, pursue it whole-heartedly. However, if it will have a negative impact on any of the creatures with which we are sharing the earth, or to the environment, then re-think it and endeavor to pursue other options.

With regards to paying attention to your innermost desire, perhaps the most famous poem (quoted below) which relate to choices is *The Road Not Taken* by Robert Frost.

Two roads diverged in a yellow wood,
And sorry I could not travel both
And be one traveler, long I stood
And looked down one as far as I could
To where it bent in the undergrowth;

Then took the other, as just as fair,
And having perhaps the better claim,
Because it was grassy and wanted wear;
Though as for that the passing there
Had worn them really about the same.

And both that morning equally lay
In leaves no step had trodden black.
Oh, I kept the first for another day!
Yet knowing how way leads on to way,
I doubted if I should ever come back.

I shall be telling this with a sigh
Somewhere ages and ages hence:
Two roads diverged in a wood, and I—
I took the one less traveled by,
And that has made all the difference.

Frost chose the path which most people did not walk on, and found it very rewarding. Do you choose your own path, or do you follow the crowd?

Regarding the choice of your journey in life which matches your deepest wishes, the quote from Ralph Waldo Emerson who wrote, "I will do strongly before the sun and moon whatever only rejoices me and the heart appoints," is very apt.

Resolve to go through life making the correct choices, even if they are difficult. The right choices will enrich your life, the lives of the people with whom you come in contact, and preserve our environment for future generations.

24 BE YOUR OWN BEST FRIEND

One of my friends pointed out to me that iron is a very hard substance, but that it can be destroyed by its own rust. Similarly, we can be agents of our own destruction. Or we can decide to be our own best friends.

In their very popular book, *How to Be Your Own Best Friend,* Mildred Newman and Bernard Berkowitz talk about being our own best friends in many areas of our lives.

Happiness. Most people are passive and hope that something, will happen to make them happy. We have to realize that we have to work at happiness. Do not look outside for your own happiness or success, but realize that the source is within you, and strive to achieve it.

Many will go to a great deal of trouble to learn French, for example, but will not take any time, or make the effort to learn about themselves. Learn what makes you happy, and be your own best friend by doing things that make you happy.

Taking Control. Most people are operating way below capacity, because they always have low expectations of themselves, very often based on the feedback of others.

We must realize that we have total control of our lives, and that we are accountable only for ourselves for what happens to us in our lives. Let us be our own best friends, and make the best use of our God-given talents.

Feelings. We have to learn to stop blaming others for the way that we feel, and realize that we are responsible for our feelings. How often we say, "This feeling just came over me."

We can choose how we feel, because our thoughts determine our feelings and we can choose what we think. If you find yourself thinking negative thoughts, you can just simply change the channel and think of something more positive.

Many times, I find myself thinking of negative things I have done, or the good things that I did not do. When this happens, I tell myself, "I am not a robot, and nobody has programmed this thought in my mind. I can change it. And I will change it."

At first, it may require a great deal of effort to do this, but it becomes easier as you do it. Now, I do it almost automatically whenever I find myself giving energy to a negative thought.

This simple act has changed my world. Norman Vincent Peale said, "Change your thoughts, and you change your world." This is because how you perceive the world depends on how you think.

Actions. Many people are literally their worst enemies. Many people do things that they know will make them feel terrible about themselves, thereby destroying themselves by their own actions. Instead, they can choose to do the things that make them feel good.

Why should you do what gives you pain, when it is just as easy to do things that give you joy? Do not be destroyed by your own rust.

Caring for Yourself. The bible says, "Love thy neighbor as thyself." It doesn't say, "better than," or "instead of." This means that you must take care of yourself, because if you don't take care of yourself, you cannot take care of others. When you are flying in an airplane, the hostess tells you that in case of an oxygen failure, you should put on your own mask first before helping others. The reason for this is quite simple. If you should lose consciousness, you cannot help anybody.

The Feeling of Helplessness. We come into this world totally helpless and very dependent. But when we grow into adulthood, many of us do not let go of that feeling of helplessness and dependence, and the need to please others.

To be your own best friend, let go of those feelings of helplessness and dependence and realize that you are the architect of your future.

Achievements. We have to realize that when we achieve, we do not take anything away from others. The world is full of abundance, and there is enough for everyone. Let us take pleasure in the achievements of others, and realize that we do not take anything away from anybody when we achieve something. Similarly, they do not take anything away from us when they achieve.

To sum up, we frequently go out of our way to please our friends. And very often we should. However, we must remember that we are our own best friends, and we must make a commitment to choose our actions and thoughts which are good for us.

25 THERE ARE NO MISTAKES—ONLY LESSONS

It is very important that we regard our mistakes as lessons and learn from them. Most of us have made numerous mistakes over the course of our lives, and our successes or failures depend on how we react to those mistakes. Did we learn from them, or did we cry and moan over them without any learning?

Most people learn more from their failures than from their successes. I know that this is true for me. When I succeed, I celebrate and savor my success. People who are close to me will believe me when I say that sometimes I have to force myself to stop celebrating. Very often my family and friends tell me, "Enough celebrating! Come back to reality now." On the other hand, when I fail, I analyze the situation, try to figure what I did wrong, and learn from my mistakes.

At eighty-two, I'm using the *Duo Lingo* program to learn French and Spanish and I make repeated mistakes. Whenever this happens, I get a message from *Duo Lingo*, "Even when you make mistakes, you're still learning."

How insightful!

Many famous people emphasized that they regarded mistakes as lessons from which they learned

For example, when Thomas Edison was asked how he felt after failing so many times to find a material that would give light without burning out he replied, "I have not failed. I've just found 10,000 ways that won't work."

Michael Jordan, the famous basketball star, said, "I've missed more than 9000 shots in my career. I've lost 300 games. I've failed over and over. And that's why I've succeeded."

Edison and Jordan learned from their mistakes and made changes that enabled them to succeed.

Children do it naturally. Take a child learning to walk for example. If, after she falls down the first time, she tells herself, "I fell down. I'm not going to try THAT again," she will never learn to walk.

Instead, without verbalizing it, the child is willing to make as many mistakes as it takes to learn to walk. Without any conscious thought, she adjusts her balance, her gait and the numerous factors involved in walking. Her learning and the resulting adjustments enable her to eventually walk without falling.

The pilot of an airplane flying from the Pearson International Airport in Mississauga to the Cheddi Jagan Airport in Guyana uses a compass. But the airplane does not fly in a straight line. Instead, it frequently goes off course and is guided back to its correct path. After a series of mistakes and corrections it eventually reaches its destination. The same is true of our lives. We are off course for a great deal of the time, but we correct ourselves in our journey towards our goals.

If we are afraid of making mistakes, or experiencing failures, we won't venture out to try new things, or persist in our goals. This failure to do can be our biggest mistake, because if we don't try, we will never have a chance to succeed.

Wayne Gretzy, a well-known hockey player, is

reputed to have said, "You miss 100% of the shots you didn't take."[4]

The first step in learning from your mistakes is recognizing that you made a mistake. If you do not want to acknowledge this fact to others, at least admit it to yourself. This is a difficult thing to do for some people who tend to blame others when things go wrong. Why is it so difficult to acknowledge that we are humans, and therefore fallible?

If we blame others, we will not examine our own thinking and behaviors and we will not feel a need to change what we do. This means that we will continue to make the same mistakes and be surprised when we get the same results. Einstein said that the definition of insanity is "doing the same thing over and over again and expecting different results."

Eventually, you will have to learn from your mistakes and change your behavior. In her wonderful book, *IF LIFE is GAME, THESE are the RULES,* Cherie Carter-Scott tells us, "Lessons will be repeated to you in various forms until you have learned them."

We can make a conscious choice to learn from our mistakes, or we can take the painful route and continue making the same mistakes until we are forced to learn from them. But eventually, we have to learn what we did wrong and change our behavior.

As we navigate through life and our paths are full of obstacles, let us acknowledge and learn from our mistakes. Our lives will be filled with learning, one of

---

[4] *Wayne Gretzky's Quotes,* Google

which is that we will continue to make mistakes and learn from them.

26 FOCUS ON WHAT YOU WANT

If we want to succeed in life, it is important that we focus on what we want, not on what we don't want. This is because our brains are very complex, and when we give attention to something, the brain focuses on it whether it is something we want or don't want. What we focus on will materialize.

To give an example of how the brain works: if I ask you not to think of the color "blue," what color are you thinking of?

One Saturday morning I was going to Tim Hortons to buy muffins, and my wife told me in a firm voice, "Make sure that you do not buy chocolate muffins."

As I was negotiating the traffic on the way to buy the muffins, I kept reminding myself, "Do not buy chocolate muffins. Do not buy chocolate muffins. Chocolate muffins, chocolate muffins."

Guess what I bought!

You're right! Chocolate muffins.

One of the survival jobs I had when I first migrated to Toronto was as a security guard at a prominent bank. The bank had signs all over the building, saying, "IN CASE OF A FIRE, DO NOT PANIC."

I advised them to change it to, "IN CASE OF A FIRE, KEEP CALM," because the occupants of the building should be thinking of calmness, rather than of panic in the event of a fire. I am pleased to say that the bank accepted my advice and changed the signs.

Mother Teresa acted on the same principle when she said, "I was once asked why I don't participate in anti-war demonstrations. I replied that I will never do that, but as soon as you have a pro-peace rally, I'll be there."

That is why in meditation and visualization exercises we are advised to see ourselves as we want to be, not as we don't want to be. If we are ill, we are led to visualize ourselves as being healthy. Over time the brain will accept this message and work towards health.

As far as the brain is concerned, "Attention means intention," and it will work to achieve what you focus on.

In affirmation activities we are led to repeat positive affirmations frequently, very often using the phrase, "I am." If you tell the brain that you are already healthy, calm, successful or whatever you want to be, it will work towards making whatever you tell it a reality.

Vadim Zeland, author of *Reality Transurfing,* advises us, "The stronger your desire to avoid something, the more likely it is that you will encounter it. To actively fight against what you do not want in your life is to make every effort to ensure that it is present in your life."

This truth is emphasized in the bible when Job says, "The thing which I greatly feared is come upon me, and that which I was afraid of is come unto me." (Job 3:25)

So, what should we do when we want to avoid something? Zeland advises, "Unless there are obvious threats or risks, what you don't like should be ignored, that is, it should never be given mental energy."

When you find yourself thinking of what you don't want, remember that you have the power to change the channel immediately, and focus on what you do want. It is important to know that you have the power to choose what you elect to think of. Remember the words of Michael Losier, a self-help advocate, "I attract into my life whatever I give my attention, energy and focus to, whether positive or negative."

As you live your everyday life then, ensure that you focus on what you want in life. Imprint your goals firmly in your mind, and watch your life unfold like the wings of a butterfly.

27 THE SELF-FULFILLING PROPHESY

Johann Wolfgang von Goethe, the German philosopher and writer, wrote, "Treat people as if they were what they ought to be and you help them to become what they are capable of becoming."

Patricia McGreer's revealing story, "Johnny's Eight-Cow wife," which was published in the 1965 edition of *Women's Day* magazine, illustrates this concept beautifully.

McGreer wrote that in Johnny's culture, a man had to give the father of the girl he wanted to marry a dowry of several cows for his daughter's hand in marriage. Two or three cows would get a man a fair wife, and four or five a very desirable one. Tradition dictated that eight cows was the largest number to be offered.

Johnny had the reputation of being a very smart trader, and wanted to marry a girl named Sarita. Sarita was extremely shy, skinny, not at all beautiful, and walked with her shoulders hunched. People said that it was a kindness to call her plain and thought that her father, Sam Karoo, would be lucky to get more than one or two cows for his daughter.

However, one day Johnny walked up to Sam Karoo. "For your daughter, Sarita, I will give you eight cows."

And Johnny proceeded to treat Sarita as an eight-cow wife.

After some time, the narrator of the story went to visit

Johnny and Sarita. The following is his description of her. "She was the most beautiful woman I have ever seen…This girl had an ethereal loveliness that was at the same time from the heart of nature. The dew-fresh flowers with which she'd pinned back her lustrous black hair accented the glow of her cheeks. The lift of her eyes all spelled a pride to which no one could deny her the right. And as she turned to leave, she moved with the grace that made her look like a queen."

The narrator was surprised and asked Johnny what happened. Did he take another wife?

Johnny replied, "No, that is Sarita. Do you ever think," he asked reflectively, "what it does to a woman when she knows that the dowry her husband paid for her is the lowest price that he can give to her father? And later, when the women talk and boast of the dowry their husbands gave for them, one says four cows, another maybe six. How does she feel—the women whose father was offered the dowry of only one or two cows? This could not happen to my Sarita."

Johnny went on to say that he wanted Sarita, and no other woman. "And I wanted an eight-cow wife."

Here is another example to illustrate the concept of the self-fulfilling prophecy. In 1968, two researchers, Rosenthal and Jacobson, administered a standardized test to students in one school. They then selected 20% of the students at random and told the teachers that these children were expected to be spurters. When the children were tested several times subsequently, the researchers found that the students who were expected to be spurters exceeded the control group in achievement. The researchers concluded that the students did so well because their teachers treated them as successful students. They stated that it was a self-fulling prophecy.

In George Bernard Shaw's play, *Pygmalion,* which was made into a film, *My Fair Lady*, the protagonist, Henry Higgins attempts to transform a flower girl, Eliza, into an aristocrat by changing her speech. He succeeds in changing her speech, but still treats her as a flower girl, and Eliza tells him, "The difference between a lady and a flower girl is not how she behaves, but how she's treated."

I can relate to this phenomenon. In Guyana, I was a captain in the army and ADC to the President. At cocktail parties and other social events, many people tried to get my attention and talk with me. Because of how I was treated, I was very proud and walked with a swagger even when I was not in uniform.

When I immigrated to Canada, I started working as a security guard earning the minimum wage, and later as a messenger at the Royal Bank of Canada. People looked down on me and treated me in a demeaning manner. For example, when I was a security guard, my supervisor handed me a bunch of keys with the admonition, "Don't lose them now."

I could not help thinking of all the responsibilities I had as an army officer, only to be cautioned by a supervisor in a security company not to lose a bunch of keys.

At parties hosted by the bank, the women would not dance with me, because I was "just a messenger," and in my social life, many of my friends and acquaintances boasted about their jobs and how much they earned. One person even flashed his paycheck and told me in a mocking voice, "You were a captain in Guyana; you're not a captain here."

I cannot find the words to explain how the way I was treated affected my self-concept. I started to question my own abilities. My thinking and behavior changed, and I began to think of myself in terms of how people treated me. Always a heavy drinker, I began to drink even more, with the consequent change in my behavior, and began to sink in the depths of despair.

The lines I wrote in the poem entitled, "My Odyssey," which was published in *Roraima: An anthology of poetry from emerging Caribbean Canadian Writers,* do not even begin to capture the anguish and despair I felt because of the treatment I received by my colleagues at work, and by my acquaintances and relatives, some of whom I had helped in Guyana:

> *Am I the person people see?*
> *Or am I the person existing in my own mind?*
> *Tiredness descends like a liquid ceiling.*
> *I have circumnavigated myself,*
> *But the truth remains undiscovered.*
> *Who am I in this slush-covered street?*

It took a great deal of effort to remind myself that I was the same person I was in Guyana, and that eventually I would succeed.

My advice to readers: treasure everyone and treat them with respect and in a manner that will bring out the best in them. In particular, treat your loved ones as precious jewels, and make them feel valued.

And yes! Treat yourself as a gem. You are one of God's creations, and you are beautiful and treasured.

28 TO UNDERSTAND ALL IS TO FORGIVE ALL

Leo Tolstoy, the prominent Russian writer, wrote, "One must put oneself in every one's position. To understand everything is to forgive everything."

The following story illustrates the above concept:

A man had a pet parrot which he loved very much. One day, he was very thirsty, and saw liquid dropping from the rocks above. He set his cup and collected the liquid until there was enough for him to drink. Just as he raised the cup to his lips, the parrot flew up, grabbed the cup with its feet, and spilled all the liquid.

Patiently, the man set the cup to collect the still dripping liquid. The same thing happened when there was enough liquid to drink the second time around.

When the parrot upset the cup the second time, the man was so thirsty and enraged that he killed the parrot. Then, because he could wait no longer to collect the liquid drop by drop, he decided to climb the rocks, to find the source of the water. When he reached the top, he saw that the liquid was poison dropping from a dragon's mouth and realized that he had killed the parrot which had saved his life.

The other illustration comes from real life.

I was surprised when my neighbor, Susan, who is a very kind and helpful woman, told me that she would never talk to Ann, the wife of a friend of mine.

When I asked her what happened, she told me that she had told Ann, "Good morning," the previous day and that Ann's response was, "What's so effing good about it?"

I explained to Susan that Ann had knee replacements, and that she saw her on the first day that she was able to walk after the surgery. Susan exclaimed, "Oh my God! I had a friend who had knee replacement surgery, and I can imagine how much pain Ann was feeling. I will reach out to her."

Susan visited Ann with a bunch of flowers and some food, and now they are the best of friends.

It is also true that many people act in a certain manner because it is simply embedded in their personalities. In 1968, Don Lowry created a program which he named *True Colors*. The program encouraged participants to identify themselves with different colors—blue, green, orange and gold—associated with specific behaviors. I will not describe the dominant behaviors associated with each color, but will elaborate on the one relevant to this passage. My older brother identified with green, and people who belong to this color group are usually obsessed with ideas. In fact, they are so focused on ideas that they generally neglect to nurture relationships.

The following story may seem far-fetched but it is true. My brother and I migrated to Toronto late in life with our families, and one evening after quite a few drinks I called him and facetiously complained, "I don't think that anybody loves me anymore."

He replied, "I love you. Your brother loves you."

His wife, who was nearby, took the phone and told me, "Ask him if he ever told me that."

When I asked my brother if he ever told his wife that he loved her he replied, "She doesn't know that? Why she thinks I married her?" Then he elaborated, "We have five children."

The reader must bear in mind that the society we grew up in was not very expressive about personal feelings.

As far as my brother was concerned, his actions were enough to prove that he loved his wife, and he didn't need to verbalize the fact. An understanding of his personality will help others gain insights into his behavior, although they may not agree with it.

How many times did people do things to help us, or prevent us from doing things that would have put us in danger, but we resented them because we didn't understand the reasons for their actions? Think of the tough decisions made by your parents when you were very young.

Did you agree with all of them? Your parents had a better understanding of the world than you did and acted in your best interests although sometimes you might have disagreed with them.

In the same way, our children may not agree with all the decisions we have made, or are making, because their understanding of the world is still in the formative stages.

When a child tells his parent, "I hate you. You're the worst father ever," the parent understands that the child is talking from a perspective of incomplete or inaccurate knowledge, and he does not love the child less.

Similarly, we are only human and we do not have the total picture. To come to the realization that we are not omniscient, and we don't know everything, is very liberating. We may not agree with all the decisions that God makes for us, because we do not have a full perspective. Only God does.

When a person verbally attacks us, if we can see the oneness that unites us all, we see the attacker as someone crying out for love. Our first instinct is to protect ourselves, and very often we should. In the long term, however, we should try to understand the experiences to which the attacker had been exposed, and forgive him.

One reason I like writing: it prompts me to get into the minds of the characters in my books, to understand why they do what they do.

What about understanding and forgiving ourselves? Many people readily forgive others, but have difficulties forgiving themselves.

Remember that you are your own best friend, and you need to forgive yourself as you would forgive your best friend. This does not mean making excuses for your behavior, but understanding your state of mind when you did, or did not say or do something. Forgive yourself, then make amends if your words or behavior caused harm to anyone, and move on.

None of us is, or will be perfect. "Progress, not perfection," is the key phrase in trying to understand why we and other people behave in specific ways as we embark on our journey called life. This understanding will inevitably lead to the forgiveness of others and of ourselves.

29 HE IS RICH WHO KNOWS HE HAS ENOUGH

Many writers emphasize the fact a person does not have to have a great deal of money to consider himself rich.

The Greek philosopher, Democritus, said, "By desiring little, a poor man makes himself rich."

Lao Tze, the famous Chinese philosopher, espoused the same ideology when he observed, "He who knows he has enough is rich."

The quote, *The richest man is not he who has the most, but he who needs the least,* is attributed to the writer, Laura Ingall Wilder.

Having enough is important, but for a person to be content it is crucial for him to KNOW that he has enough. It is possible for a person to have more than enough, but if he still feels that he needs more, he is clinging to the mentality of poverty—of always wanting. Such a person is always striving to grasp more and is constantly in a state of dis-ease and dissatisfaction.

Many psychologists would agree that the person who has enough, but still feels the need to acquire more and more wealth often at the expense of personal relationships, has a deep void within that he is trying to fill. No amount of money will fill this void, and he is likely to trample on the rights of others to acquire more and more wealth.

For example, I know someone who lives in Richmond Hill, which is an exclusive area in the Greater Toronto Area. He has a very large and beautiful home and is quite wealthy. Yet, whenever I called him he always complained of how he was cheated by someone he knew, or how he was wrongly accused by one of his friends of borrowing money and not paying it back, or of some incident related to money or possessions. He would swear loudly during his diatribes, and I prayed that none of my children would pick up the phone while I was talking with him. I stopped calling him after a while.

The Bible warns us about the accumulation of wealth at the expense of sacrificing one's personal values. Mark, 8: 36 exhorts us, "For what shall it profit a man, if he shall gain the whole world, and lose his own soul?"

Then, there is the kind of person who will go to great lengths to ostentatiously display his wealth, although doing so makes it difficult for him and his family to enjoy the everyday pleasures of life.

This type of person is described by Rabindranath Tagore: "The child who is decked with prince's robes and who has jeweled chains round his neck loses all pleasure in his play; his dress hampers him at every step."

Tagore continued. "Mother, it is no gain, thy bondage of finery, if it keeps one shut off from the healthful dust of the earth, if it robs one of the right of entrance to the great fair of human life."

It's time for us to rethink the concept of wealth. Of course, our physical bodies must be taken care of, but if we have enough resources to take care of our basic human needs we are rich, and it is important that we know and accept this fact.

We can sleep in only one bed at any given time, and we don't often need more than three meals a day. How many people in Western countries eat more than they should, and go on diets to lose weight? A large percentage of the population of the world has health problems because of overeating and the abuse of alcohol and other drugs, while a large percentage of the population is starving.

As far as clothing is concerned, how many people have wardrobes full of clothes that they have never worn, or wore only once? How many people go shopping for clothes, not because they are in need, but because they want to wear the latest style?

Often, we are not aware of how much we have, and therefore are not grateful for our possessions. To make my students aware of all their blessings, I often asked them this question, "Would you trade what you have for a hundred million dollars?"

All of them would answer, "No!"

Then I would ask, "How about a billion dollars? Would you trade your ability to walk, to talk, to see, to smell for a billion dollars?"

They would all shake their heads to indicate the negative, and I would emphasize how blessed we are.

To be rich, we do not need to have large bank accounts, and we do not have to display our fine clothes, or impressive houses. If we know that we have enough, we are rich.

30 BEING KIND IS IMPORTANT

F. Scott Fitzgerald, author of *The Great Gatsby* and other books, observed, "To be kind is more important than to be right. Many times, what people need is not a brilliant mind that speaks but a special heart that listens." In our lives, it is important for us to be kind to others instead of proving to them how *right* we are if this act causes harm to others.

The following verse, from Dale Carnegie's *How to Stop Worrying and Start Living,* demonstrates the harm we can cause ourselves and others when we egotistically act on the feeling of being *right*:

John Bright was a citizen
Of credit and renown
Dead right as he sped along
But he's just as dead as if he were wrong.

For those of us who are drivers, in order to avoid an accident, how many times have we given way to other drivers who were obviously in the wrong,? Out of a sense of self-preservation, we recognized that it was better to give way than to prove we were *right*.

Needless to say, the struggle to be right affects your health and well-being because when you argue with another person, and your desire to be right kicks in, your body gets in the *fight or flight* mode causing it to be suffused with adrenaline. There is a consequent unhealthy change of the chemistry of the entire body which moves into the "high alert" stage.

However, if you choose to be kind, the body relaxes and produces serotonin, which has a calming effect.

Many holy books are full of references to the value of kindness.

Proverbs 21, verse 21, in the Bible advises us that "Kindness is no small thing. It yields marvelous fruit both in our lives and the lives of those around us. Whoever pursues righteousness and kindness will find life, righteousness, and honor."

And the Koran exhorts us to, "…be kind to parents, relatives, orphans, the poor, near and distant neighbors, close friends …Surely Allah does not like whoever is arrogant, boastful."

Often, we don't know what struggles another person is experiencing when we wrestle to assert our rights. For example, in the school where I taught, a junior teacher, who was not qualified to teach the course I taught, was given preference over me to teach that course. I was enraged and wanted to protest to the Teachers' Federation and even take legal action if necessary, but I consulted with two friends before I lodged a formal protest.

The first friend was the head of guidance in the same school. He advised me, "Ken, I can't share all the details with you, but believe me, you will do a kindness to Ann if you don't complain to the Federation."

When I consulted with my other friend he counseled, "I know that you are a kind person. From what you told me, you will win this case with the Federation, but do you really want to protest? Think of what it will do to the other teacher. You are qualified to teach other subjects, so you won't be out of a job." Then he concluded with an observation which led to the title of this meditation. "In my life, I have always found that it is better to be kind than to be *right*."

I did not lodge a complaint and learned later that the teacher who was given preference over me had stage four cancer, and had confidentially shared this information with the administration who gave her a schedule she could manage, enabling her to work for as long as she was able. She passed away about eighteen months later.

I cannot find the words to express my relief that I chose to be kind rather than to be *right* in this instance.

It is easy to let our sense of importance and confidence in our knowledge prompt us to show others how right we are, but most of us will find that kindness will trump the feeling of being right any time.

31 YOU ARE YOUR WORST CRITIC

Many of us are our own worst critics and focus on the negative aspects of our lives.

Many good things must have happened in our lives for us to be where we are, but for one reason or another, many of us focus on the negative incidents. I know that this is true for me, and that I am my most severe and frequent critic. I suspect that the same is true for many of you.

Ethan Kross, author of *The Voice in our Head, Why It Matters, and How to Harness It* observes that "negative chatter can undermine our ability to think and perform. It can create problems in our relationships, and also has the potential to undermine our physical health." He stresses that "negative self-talk can fuel our stress response, which can lead to sleep disorders, and an increased incidence of cardiovascular illness."

But there is hope. We can manage the critic in our heads. The first thing to do is to be aware of what you are telling yourself. Don't judge yourself! Just be aware, because when you judge, you are giving energy to the behavior of self-criticism that you are trying to change.

Notice what triggers your inner critic. Do you do it when you are tired? Or when you're angry? Or just before you go to sleep?

Kross suggests that whenever you tend to indulge in negative self-talk, you should mentally and emotionally detach yourself from the situation, and imagine that you are giving advice to your best friend. Would you be as harsh to your best friend as you are to yourself?

You can also get outside yourself and look at nature, at a beautiful sunset, or children playing without a care in the world. When you observe the beauty and awe of nature, you come to the realization that as a part of nature, you are valued and valuable.

Many people find that volunteering to help others, for example in a hospital, will help shift their attention from themselves to others who are less fortunate than themselves.

Ekhart Tolle in his book, *The Power of Now,* suggests a deeper approach. He compares his strategy to the process of alchemy—changing base metal into gold—and advises that when you find yourself thinking negative thoughts, stop giving energy to that thought, and use the negative thought as a trigger to go deeply into your body. Feel your life's energy flowing through your body, from head to toe, from toe to head. It is this energy that is keeping you alive. A recently deceased body has the same molecules as a living one, but is lacking the energy that you feel when you go deeply into your body.

In this manner, you transform the negative thought into something positive. After a while, you will begin to welcome the incipient negative thought, because you know that you will transform it into a positive experience by going deep inside your body.

Body awareness also has other benefits. Tolle says that it will ward off many diseases, and observes that if the owner of the house does not inhabit the house, unwanted guests will enter.

I have tried the process described above and can attest to the fact that it works although it takes some practice.

If you forget sometimes to employ the transformation process when you think negative thoughts, forgive yourself. None of us is perfect. Do it whenever you remember, and after a while the process will become automatic.

Shad Helmstetter wrote a beautiful book, *What to Say When You Talk to Yourself.* Helmstetter advises us that if we must talk to ourselves, we might as well make a conscious decision to tell ourselves good things.

One of the ways to do this is to develop a set of affirmations which we constantly repeat to ourselves, especially when we find ourselves thinking negative thoughts. After some time, they will automatically become part of our thinking.

One of my affirmations is, "I am filled with love and peace. I forgive myself and others for errors of the past. I am healthy and well." I repeat this when I go for walks, before I go to sleep, and when negative thoughts threaten to disturb my peace of mind.

Use whatever strategies work for you. The results are worth the effort. After a while, you will find that you criticize yourself less and less. Instead, you will remind yourself that you are a beautiful human being who deserves a great deal of love and respect.

32 IF YOU THINK YOU CAN, YOU'RE RIGHT

Many people handicap themselves by convincing themselves they cannot perform certain tasks, and they consequently avoid those tasks. However, very often, we can do more than we think that we can. Some psychologists and prominent people affirm that most people are not achieving their full potential because they underestimate their own abilities. Henry Ford observed, "Whether you think you can, or you think you can't—you're right."

A self-improvement coach, Rolle Edema, told us much the same thing in different words when she said, "One of the primary ways of getting what you want out of life, is firstly to start believing that you can achieve what you set your mind to."

We often hear of people performing seemingly impossible feats under hypnosis, because the hypnotist suggests that they can perform specific tasks. For example, we have heard or have read about people lifting heavy objects to free a loved one who was trapped, because they told themselves that they could do it. The brain is so wonderful that it believes what it is told and sends corresponding messages to the body.

However, we don't have to wait for a hypnotist to tell us what we can, or cannot do. We hypnotize ourselves every day by telling ourselves that we can do certain things, or that we can't do those things.

And of course, in either case we prove ourselves right. If we tell ourselves that we are too old, too busy, or that we don't have a particular skill to do something, our brains will prove us right.

On the other hand, if we tell ourselves that we will succeed in doing or achieving something regardless of the obstacles, we will also prove ourselves right.

In one of my earlier meditations, I discussed the self-fulling prophecy and outlined the situation in which students performed better than their classmates because their teacher expected them to excel. We also have expectations of ourselves and we tell ourselves that we will be successful or that we won't, and the self-fulfilling prophecy comes into effect. Do you tell yourself that you can succeed in something you want to do? Or do you tell yourself that you can't?

Very often family members, relatives or close friends tell us that we can, or can't do something. We can choose to believe them or we can tell ourselves the opposite. In the movie, *The Pursuit of Happyness*, Will Smith tells his son, "Never let people tell you that you can't do something. You can do anything that you put your mind to."

Shad Helmstetter, in his insightful book, *What to Say When You Talk to Yourself,* compares our minds to computer programs, and observes that many of us have been programmed from our childhood to believe that we can't do certain things. However, Helmstetter insists that it is never too late to change the programs and advises, "You can reprogram. You can erase the negative, counter-productive, work-against-you programming and replace it with a healthy, new, positive, *productive* kind of programming. And it's easy. *Erase and replace.* All you have to do is learn how to talk to yourself."

Phillip McGraw, in his book *Self Matters,* echoes Helmstetter when he describes his experiences when he tried to assemble a swing set. McGraw told himself, "You are so screwed here! You don't have a snowball's chance in hell of ever getting this put together by Christmas morning. You'd better get Scott (my brother-in-law, who has some kind of weird "engineering" brain parts I just didn't get) out of bed..."

What are the chances that I would have the same experience as McGraw? I had bought a swing set and automatically called my brother-in-law to help me assemble it, because I had previously convinced myself that I did not have the skills to complete a task like this. I had told myself that I was not coordinated, and that my brain did not allow me to assemble objects. However, my brother-in-law was not available and I was forced to reprogram myself. I told myself, "I am a reasonably intelligent, able-bodied man. The instructions for assembling the swing are quite clear, and I am a good reader. Besides, all the tools required for assembling the swing are included in the package. I can do it."

I rolled up my sleeves, took a few deep breaths, started the seemingly impossible task, and I surprised myself by assembling the set single-handedly. Of course, this increased my self-confidence and I started to take on other tasks which I would have depended on my brother-in-law to complete.

In earlier civilizations, people were stuck in different classes—the monarchy, nobility, priests, peasants, etc.— and had to remain in those roles to preserve a sense of order. Today, our structures are more fluid, and people are no longer expected to be confined to occupations which define their identities and their names, e.g. Smith, Farmer. However, many people remain conditioned by close family members and by society and continue to limit themselves by telling themselves that they can't do certain things. The individuals who did not accept this conditioning and have broken out of the mold which was cast around them are to be admired for paving the way for future generations.

While I was writing this passage, I serendipitously picked up a copy of an ethnic magazine, *Share*. This magazine describes the process in which Lawrence Hill, the author of *The Book of Negroes* and other books, was enrolled at The University of Toronto Schools. When he applied to get into the school, his father told him, "You are not getting into that school," because he was Black, but Lawrence Hill was determined and told himself that he would succeed in his attempt to gain admittance to this exclusive school.

His determination led to his acceptance into the University of Toronto Schools, and when he shared his experiences with reporters he noted, "I was the only Black student in my Grade, and often the only one in the school." Hill noted that the school has been more inclusive since.

Lawrence Hill's experiences bring to mind the challenges encountered by women and racial and ethnic minority groups when they try to be hired for certain jobs, or even to gain admittance in some social clubs. Kudos to those who told themselves that they could do it, and by succeeding, opened the doors for others.

These pioneers knew what they wanted to do and relentlessly pursued their goals, thus observing Deepak Chopra's concept of dharma—our purpose in life. Chopra emphasized that, regardless of what society or the people close to you tell you what you can or can't do, if you can discover your dharma and pursue it, you are blessed.

So, my advice to my readers is to be very careful what you tell yourselves, because if you tell yourselves that you can, or that you can't, you will prove yourself right. And this will determine how your future infolds.

33 EQUITY FOR WOMEN

I had some doubts about writing a passage related to the rights of women and asked myself, "What gives me the right to talk about equity for women?"

So I called my brother, Dwarka, who is the founder of *the New Millenium Ministries,* and asked his advice. He reminded me that, as a man, I belong to a group which has discriminated against women for centuries, and many women are still being discriminated against in our society. He stressed that, as a member of the group discriminating against women, I am part of the problem. I should also be part of the solution.

A discussion of the history of discrimination against women is important for two reasons. First, we have to learn from history. George Santayana, Spanish-American philosopher, poet and playwright, said, "Those who do not learn from history are doomed to repeat it." These words were later quoted by Winston Churchill during World War 2.

The second reason is one of hope. When we look at the history of discrimination against women, and women's struggle for equality, we can see how far we have come. This does not mean that we have to be complacent. There is much more to be done to achieve full equality, but we can do so with hope.

Until the mid-nineteenth century, women typically did not hold property or appear as *persons* before the law. As a matter of fact, a wife was considered the property of her husband, and a daughter the property of her father.

We still recognize this phenomenon when a woman gets married in the Christian religion. Usually the father walks with the bride to the altar, and during the ceremony the priest asks, "Who giveth this woman to this man?" The father replies, "I do!"

So in the past, the woman moved from becoming the property of her father to becoming the property of her husband.

As far as suffrage is concerned, it was not until 1920 that the United States ratified the 19th Amendment, giving women the right to vote. This was after many women like Elizabeth Cady Stanton, Susan B. Anthony, Ida B. Wells, and Lucretia Mott campaigned tirelessly for the right to vote. Organizing for women's suffrage dated back to 1848, and the Seneca Falls Convention is reported to be the first women's rights conference in the United States.

In 1928, the Supreme Court of Canada ruled that women were not "persons" according to the British North America Act (now called the Constitution Act, 1867). Therefore, they were ineligible for appointment to the Senate. However, the Judicial Committee of the Privy Council reversed the Court's decision on 18th October 1929.

The Persons Case (*Edwards v. A.G. of Canada*) established the right of women to be appointed to the Senate and enabled women to work for change in both the House of Commons and the Senate. This landmark ruling meant that women could no longer be denied rights based on a narrow interpretation of the law.

The denial of women to participate in crucial areas of society is in spite of the fact that women played prominent roles such as judges, prophets, and doctors in the Bible.

Judges, chapter 4 and 5, tells us about Deborah, who stepped into the position of a judge, a position held only by men. She went into battle with her people to fight for freedom from a cruel Canaanite king, Sisera. When Sisera was killed, Israel had peace for forty years.

Then we have Esther, whom the Persian king. Xerxes had chosen as his wife. Esther did not reveal her Jewish heritage, and when the king's advisor, Haman, planned to exterminate the Jews, Esther went before Xerxes, and pleaded with him to save her people. In doing so, she risked her life, but saved the Jews.

More recently the book, *This Day in History* records a significant event that occurred on June 4, 1913. On that day, a lady named Emily Wilding Davison was trampled by King George V's horse as she was demonstrating for the right of women to vote. Davidson died eight days later from a skull fracture.

Relating the difficulties women face in politics, Hilary Clinton, in her book *WHAT HAPPENED*, described the "impossible balancing act" women in politics face between being warm and emotional (and thus perceived as inexperienced and unable to handle the pressure of foreign diplomacy) and being thoughtful and cautious (and thus perceived as cold and unlikeable.)

Clinton wrote, "Can you blame us for feeling like we can't win, no matter what we do?"

In recent times, more women and racial minorities are being represented equitably in the workplace. Although this passage is about equity for women, I must mention the struggles of racial minorities, because this group shares the experience of discrimination with women.

During my tenure as an antiracist consultant in the East York Board of Education, I noted that most teachers in the elementary schools were women but there were only two female principals.

The Board tried to hire more female principals, and the question was asked, "Does this mean that the quality of principals will be lowered?"

One female vice-principal gave the best answer I heard, when she said, "Quality will definitely increase, instead of being lowered. In the past, the Board picked principals and vice-principals from only 50% of the population, but now it is filling these positions from 100% of the population."

I liked this answer, but I had also to point out its inaccuracy because all the female principals hired and promoted were white. So, the Board was choosing vice-principals and principals from less that 100% of the population, because women of color were ignored

The fight for equality for women is far from over, but awareness of the inequities faced by women has increased, and we must make a commitment to continue to achieve equity for women from all racial and cultural backgrounds.

34 HUMILITY

The dictionary defines humility as *a modest or low view of one's own importance; humbleness*. It is the opposite of *ego* or the belief that one's *self* is all important. Humility is crucial in our interactions with others because it reveals so much about ourselves and of our regard for others with whom we share this planet.

Cherie Carter-Scott, in her book *IF LIFE IS A GAME, THESE ARE THE RULES,* observes, "A person with humility has a confident yet modest sense of his or her own merits, but also an understanding of his or her limitations. The moment you think you have seen everything or know it all ("Been there, done that…"), the universe senses arrogance and gives you a big dose of humility."

I can relate to the above concept. When I was in Guyana and an officer in the Guyana Defence Force, I was very arrogant and conceited. The fact that people respected me and looked up to me fuelled my arrogance and conceit. Then I immigrated to Canada and started to work as a security guard. People, including those close to me, taunted me about how cushy their jobs were, how much they were earning, and pointed out, "You were a captain in the army in Guyana. You're not a captain here," as they flashed their paychecks. Thus the universe forced me to be humble and all my feelings of grandeur and self-importance evaporated.

Commenting on humility, Gandhi emphasized that

"True humility means strenuous and constant endeavour entirely directed to the service of humanity."

The New Testament in the Bible gives us a powerful lesson in humility. Jesus Christ was born in a manger, instead of in a palace and Joseph, His earthly father, was a simple carpenter. Jesus's entire life was one of simplicity and humility, but we nevertheless remember Him above kings and queens in all their splendor.

The poet, Michelle Nadasi, points out the different effects of pride and humility on a person: "Pride stunts your growth and mind/Humility spreads the wealth of all things/good and kind."

There is an important difference in acting humbly, and truly being humble. For example, I can remember going to a Christmas get-together held in the home of one of the teachers in my school. When I arrived, there were two empty chairs, but I decided to show people how humble I was, and sat on the floor, leaving the empty chairs for the latecomers. On the surface, I was acting humbly, but all the while I was thinking, "I hope that people are noticing how humble I am."

Then one young woman of Japanese background left her chair and sat beside me. I felt very special and flattered because I thought that she was attracted to me, until she turned to me and said, "If my father were to walk in here and see me sitting on a chair and an old man sitting on the floor, I'll never hear the end of it."

When I shared this story with my son and asked him if I was shortchanging myself by thinking that I was not humble, he replied, "Don't worry, dad. Believe me, you are not humble. The teacher who left her comfortable chair and sat beside you on the floor is humble. You were so proud of your self-perceived humility that you wanted to show off. She was so humble that she could not be comfortable sitting on her chair with you sitting on the floor."

Many of us perform acts of kindness towards others, expecting to be noticed and thanked. True humility means that the giver does not expect to be acknowledged. Many humble people perform acts of kindness without the receivers even knowing who was responsible. The performance of a kind and humble act is enough reward for them.

The Koran exhorts us to do good and warns us not to be boastful. "Worship Allah and associate nothing with Him, and to parents do good, and to relatives, orphans, the needy, the near neighbor, the neighbor farther away, the companion at your side, the traveler, and those whom your right hands possess. Indeed, Allah does not love those who are self-deluding and boastful."

Dale Carnegie, in his insightful book, *How to Stop Worrying and Start Living,* give this advice, "If we want to find happiness, let's stop thinking about gratitude or ingratitude and give for the inner joy of giving." He cites the example of Andrew Carnegie who gave one of his relatives one million dollars, but the relative still reviled him after his death. The reason? Andrew Carnegie had left 365 million dollars to various charities.

Let us make a commitment to strive to be humble in our service to God and to our fellow human beings while not seeking external rewards or thanks.

35 LOVE IS STRONGER THAN HATE

Love is always stronger and more effective than hate. Love is stronger than hate even when people hurt us so much that we feel we cannot forgive them.

I recently watched a television program which commemorated the incident when a Muslim family of three generations was mowed down by a truck driven by a man who hated Muslims. Five members of the multigenerational family were walking on a quiet Sunday evening when the incident occurred. Four were killed, and a nine-year-old boy ended up in the hospital with serious injuries.

The Prime Minister of Canada, the Premier of Ontario, and the mayors of Toronto and London were among the many dignitaries attending the memorial for the victims. The imam of the mosque to which the family belonged, and other spiritual leaders, were present.

Everybody in the group came together in love. People who were not related to the family expressed love for the members, and for the Muslim community, which had reason to feel threatened and afraid. The Muslim leaders and close relatives of those who were killed expressed love and gratitude for the people who supported them at that time.

Each group emphasized the statement which has stayed with me. They reiterated, "LOVE IS STRONGER

THAN HATE."

I thought deeply about the above statement: "How can relatives who had lost so many of their loved ones remain so positive?"

"What is love?" I asked myself. In this context, I am not referring to the passionate love of a man for a woman, or a woman for a man, although this too can be spiritual. I am talking about the deep and abiding love, and reverence for our fellow human beings, for all creatures on this beautiful planet, for nature, and for our planet itself.

I looked for references related to the triumph of love over hate in religious texts and self-help books, and found several potent messages about the power of love.

Paul's letter in I Corinthians 13: 13 emphasizes, "And now abide faith, hope, love, these three; but the greatest of these is love."

Matthew 5:44 exhorts us: "But I say to you, Love your enemies and pray for those who persecute you."

And Luke 6:27 tells us, "But I say to you who hear, love your enemies, do good to those who hate you."

In the *Bhagavad Gita*, Lord Krishna says, "The only way you can conquer me is through Love, and there I am gladly conquered." Krishna goes on to explain that we should recognise the divine spark that exists in everyone and love all beings.

This suggests that the seed of love is intrinsic to every human being, whereas hatred is learned and nurtured by feelings of distrust, ignorance and apprehension. When we recognize the causes of hatred, we can return to our true nature, that of pure love.

Martin Luther King Jr., in his struggle to achieve equity for Black people advised his followers, "I have decided to stick with love. Hate is too great a burden to bear…Love is the only force capable of transforming an enemy into a friend. If you are seeking the highest good, I think you can find it through love. And the beautiful thing is that we aren't moving wrong when we do it, because John was right, God is love. He who hates does not know God, but he who loves has the key that unlocks the door to the meaning of ultimate reality[5]."

In many of the previous passages, I've mentioned the link between meditation and medication. Deepak Chopra stressed that with every thought we have, a chemical is produced in our body. The feeling of love produces calming chemicals like serotonin, while feelings of hate lead to a production of adrenaline—preparing us for the *flight or fight* response. This suggests that our body is healthier when we think feelings of love rather than of hate.

How can we love everybody, even those that hate us and have done us wrong? We must realize that we are all bundles of energy, and that we all share the energy that keeps the universe vibrant. We were all once innocent children as William Wordsworth noted in his beautiful poem, *Ode: Intimations of Immortality from Recollections of Early Childhood*: "Heaven lies about us in our infancy!/Shades of the prison-house begin to close/ Upon the growing Boy."

---

[5] Excerpt from Martin Luther King Jr.'s speech "Where do we go from here."

From our heavenly infancy, we begin to have experiences, and these experiences influence our behaviors as we mature. A close friend told me that he was given a statement and advised to read whenever he felt that somebody did him wrong. The statement read, "This person had a number of negative experiences that influenced him to behave this way. How can I help him?"

My friend did this on several occasions and his focus shifted from a feeling of hate and betrayal to one of love and helpfulness. I asked him how he could feel a need to help the person who had hurt him and he replied, "I found it difficult at first, but it becomes easier every time I do it." Then he continued, "The alternative—to feel hatred and resentment—is more painful."

To go from hatred to love involves an awakening from within, because they are not superficial emotions. This takes a great deal of time but the results are well worth the effort. A person can save himself a whole lot of pain by making the effort to enable the transformation of hate to love. I have felt hatred and resentment, and later in life I have felt empathy and love for the person who had hurt me. My friend was right. Hatred is much more painful.

Sharletta Evans from Colorado was a truly enlightened soul who adopted the man, Raymond Johnson , who killed her three-year-old son. Johnson had humbly apologised to Evans who said, "I can truly say I love the young man and love him enough to take him as a son and care for him."

I still find it mind boggling that a woman would adopt a man who had killed her son, and I struggle to understand the feelings which made her do so. But her actions have led me to make a commitment to always strive to cultivate the feelings of love, instead of hate.

Sharing and experiencing love is good for us all, for every living creature, and our beautiful planet, because it is stronger than hate.

36 LET YOUR WORD BE YOUR BOND

It is important that we keep our word and that the people with whom we interact can be confident that we will do what we say we will do. We are all attracted to, and admire people who keep their word. These people are extolled in many religious and secular texts, while those who do not keep their promises are criticized.

The Koran admonishes against the breaking of promises in Chapter 61, verses 2-3: "O you who believe! Why do you say that which you do not do?"

And the Bible tells us in 1 John 2:5, "But whoever keeps his word, in him truly the love of God is perfected. By this we may know that we are in him."

Leah Bayubay, a writer and editor of *Upjourney*, a magazine for better living, in her website *Personal Growth,* writes, "When we keep our promises, we're not just ticking off a task on our to-do list; **we're nurturing trust, respect, and integrity** [her emphasis] in our relationships. It sounds simple, yet in our fast-paced world, the true art of keeping a promise seems to be fading. But what if I told you that mastering this art could be the secret to stronger relationships, a rock-solid reputation, and even personal growth?"

To demonstrate that the keeping of promises is the foundation of trust and integrity, think of a person whom you really trust. And now think of a person whom you don't trust. Why do you trust one person and distrust another?

Most likely, the person you trust always keeps his word and you can rely on him to do what he says he's going to do. On the other hand, the person you don't trust don't always do what he promised to do, and this leaves you in a state of anxiety.

As Bayubay observed, keeping your word is central to your integrity. We all know people who have a habit of just throwing words in the air that they have no intention of honoring. Sometimes they say what they think the other person wants to hear. Or they say "Yes" to a request you made because they don't want to hurt your feelings. But when they don't do what they promised to do, they hurt your feelings even more, and in addition they damage their integrity. After a while, we recognise these people and regard them with distrust. Had they said that they could not do something in the first place, you would have made other plans for the completion of that particular task.

Then there are some people who bargain with God when they are in a difficult situation and tell God, "Lord if you get me out of this, I'll do this, or I'll do that." However, when they get out of the situation, they forget all about their promise to God.

On the other hand, there are people who, when they tell you that they are going to do something, you know that it will be done. The people who keep their word have a deep sense of honor which they are determined to maintain and you can literally trust them with your life.

Why should you keep your word? When others know they can rely on you, they are more willing to associate with you because you are predictable. This predictability increases the comfort level of your friends and acquaintances. If you are serving on a committee for example, and you are assigned a particular task, the other members of the committee will be confident that the task will be completed in a timely manner.

If somebody does not usually keep his word and is assigned a particular task. his colleagues will be in a constant state of anxiety, not knowing whether the task will be completed. Most likely, such a person will not be given important tasks crucial to the completion of a project, and it is unlikely that he will be promoted to any position which requires dependability.

The damaging chemicals that anxiety produces in the body were discussed in earlier passages. Nobody would like to have and maintain an anxiety producing relationship with someone they can't trust.

So. make a pact with yourself to keep your word. If you can't do something, say that you cannot do it, even though it may be difficult to refuse at that time. And if you say that you're going to do something, do it no matter how difficult the task.

"*... let your 'Yes' be 'Yes,' and your 'No,' 'No, '*" we are advised in Matthew 5:37.

Make your word your bond, so that you can be true to yourself and steadfast to your friends.

37 SILENCE AND STILLNESS

Silence and stillness are crucial in our lives, which are filled with all kinds of physical, emotional and mental noise. It is a struggle to stay calm when we are faced with numerous trials and problems in our fast-paced world. In addition to the physical sounds and all the activity around us, our minds make so much noise that we find it difficult to be still mentally and emotionally.

Mac Ehrmann reminds us of this turbulence and the need to be still in his *Desiderata:* "Go placidly amid the noise and haste/ and remember what peace there may be in silence."

The value of silence and stillness is also emphasized in the Bible. Psalms 46, verse 10, tells us, "Be still and know that I am God."

Many famous people practiced and extolled the virtues of silence and stillness. Gandhi designated one day in the week that he would not speak, and many spiritual leaders advise that we try to be silent for periods of time, starting with a few minutes and increasing the time as we get more comfortable with silence.

This type of silence and stillness is different from enforced silence when someone has to be alone because of circumstances beyond his control, although loneliness in this instance can also be used as a time for growth. This passage will describe the benefits of, and the need for voluntary silence and stillness.

In our everyday lives, many people are uncomfortable with the empty spaces in a conversation and feel a need to fill these spaces with words, instead of feeling comfortable with silence. Kahlil Gibran comments on this phenomenon in *The Prophet:*

> *You talk when you cease to be at peace with your thoughts;*
> *And when you can no longer dwell in the solitude of your heart you live in your lips, and sound is a diversion and a pastime.*
> *And in much of your talking, thinking is half murdered.*

I am reminded of a younger brother whom I hadn't seen for a while, and who is a pastor of a church in North Carolina. He called me one day and informed me that he would visit for a weekend. "We don't even have to say anything," he said. "We'll just sit and be with each other for a while."

We met, and of course we spoke, but I am convinced that our visit would have been just as enjoyable had we not spoken a word.

In addition to physical silence, there are also many benefits to mental and emotional silence. Most people are aware that there is a "committee" in their heads, constantly arguing and predicting outcomes, many of them negative.

Eckhart Tolle, in his insightful book, *The Power of Now,* writes: "Most of us are addicted to thinking, and don't know how to be still, and a great deal of this thinking, like emotional noise, is destructive." He suggests that we learn to quiet the mind.

Some people surmise that we have upwards of 50,000 thoughts a day. These thoughts aren't always pretty and we tell ourselves things like, "I can't believe I messed up. I'm an idiot. I can't do it. It's too hard. I'm a failure. I'm too old. I'm too young." Many people find that it is a challenge to still these thoughts and to be quiet in their minds.

That's why it's so important that we follow the example of Jesus. As a terrifying storm in the Sea of Galilee caused the disciples to fear for their lives, Jesus calmly and confidently stilled the raging water with three words: *Peace! Be still!*

Similarly, we must learn to still our minds amidst the storms in the outside world.

What happens when we are silent? The mind becomes quiet and we are aware of the silence around us.

But more than that, we are aware of something greater than ourselves as we merge into the universal energy. This experience may last for only a few moments—yogis do this for longer periods! Untrained people get only glimpses of being one with the universe, but the experience lasts longer with frequent practice.

If you're looking for peace and tranquility, begin the practice of silence and stillness. The rewards are worth the time and effort.

38 CONFLICT

As long as humans live in communities, there will always be some sort of conflict. Conflicts can be minor: which channel a couple should watch on the television on a particular evening, or can be life-determining—whether you should concede to the demands of a burglar. Perhaps the most damaging of all conflicts are the conflicts between nations which lead to wars in which millions of lives are lost.

How we deal with conflict will determine whether our lives will be peaceful and prosperous or full of strife and turmoil.

In every conflict, we have several options—*I win/you lose, I lose/you win, I lose/you lose* or *I win/you win*. The situation in which we find ourselves determines which of these options is the most appropriate one, and it is crucial that we opt for the strategy that is appropriate for that situation.

For example, if we are playing a game of checkers or baseball, it would be appropriate to strive for the I *win/you lose* situation. If, however, we are confronted on a dark street by a robber armed with a pistol, we intuitively realise that we have found ourselves in a *I lose/you win* situation and will most likely do the wise thing and hand over our wallets and valuables. Strangely, some people choose the *I lose/you lose* strategy. For example, two neighbors in the village in which I grew up argued over who should pick the coffee from one tree located right on the boundary line of their properties. The adrenaline in their bodies started flowing and neither was willing to concede, so they started fighting. One neighbor killed the other with his cutlass and ended up in jail. Regardless of who was right or who was wrong, neither of them was able to pick the coffee from the disputed tree. How much difference would the coffee from the one tree have made to their lifestyles anyway?

The ideal choice is, of course, the *I win/you win* option, where each person feels that, while he perhaps made some concessions, he has gained something and that the other person has also gained. The common saying, "Live and let live" has a great deal of merit.

Communication is the key to the *I win/you win* resolution. An example is when the buyer and seller are negotiating the cost of a house and the real estate agent goes back and forth with offers and counteroffers until a mutual agreement about the price is reached. The ideal situation is when the seller feels that he has gotten a fair price for his house and the buyer believes that he has paid a fair price for the property.

Most situations are not so simple. I was teaching a co-operative class in an adult high school where the students spent four weeks in class, discussing resume writing, interview skills, performance in the job, etc. Some students frequently came in late and fell asleep in class. I could not, in good conscience, place these students with any of the co-op supervisors who worked with me and trusted me to send them reliable students.

In my interviews with these students, I emphasized that we wanted to achieve the same goal. They wanted to succeed in the job and I wanted them to succeed, but that this would not happen if they continued with their present behavior. Frequently, the student would explain that some event/s in their lives were preventing them from giving their full attention to the program, and we would decide that the best option is for them to withdraw from the program and enrol later when their problems were resolved. On some occasions, the student decided to avoid distractions and focus on the program. In both these situations, the resolution of conflict resulted in an *I win/you win* situation.

Our personality types also determine our responses to conflict situations. There are three dominant types of personalities—passive, aggressive and assertive. It must be emphasized that each person embodies all three types of the above-mentioned personalities and uses each one in appropriate situations. There is a problem, however, if a person is always passive or aggressive.

The passive individual is of the *you're important/I'm not important* mindset and does what's best for the other person instead of considering his own needs. This strategy works best in some situations. For example. when a person is caring for a child, he should place the needs of the child above his own. However, it is not the best strategy when you are negotiating a business deal or dealing with colleagues at the office.

The aggressive person believes that the *I'm important/you're not important* strategy works for him. Such a person does not care how much others suffer, providing he gets whatever he desires. Again, this strategy may be appropriate in a sports competition, but not in business dealings, and most people will avoid doing business with aggressive individuals unless it's necessary.

The assertive person is committed to the *I'm important/you're important* philosophy, and will endeavour to arrive at a solution to a conflict that will affirm the rights of all the parties involved. The assertive person does not trample on anybody's rights, while maintaining his own rights.

As mentioned above, communication is the key to the resolution of conflicts, and it is crucial that people involved in a conflict communicate with each other. What happens when the people involved in a conflict refuse to talk to each other? The labor unions have a process to address this. When talks between the unions and the employers break down, they communicate through a mediator who goes back and forth to convey the demands/offers from the employers and labor unions. If this fails, both parties may agree to abide by the decision of a mutually agreed-upon arbitrator.

In this short passage, I am able only to cover the fundamental theory of conflict resolution. However, the key to the resolution of any conflict is regard for the other person. If we regard others as fellow human beings with whom we are privileged to share this beautiful planet, there will be fewer conflicts, and conflicts will be resolved without the loss of lives, and without depriving individuals of their dignity.

39 LIGHT A CANDLE

Darkness cannot exist in the presence of light, so instead of railing against the darkness, bring in the light. I am referring, of course, to physical darkness as well as the metaphorical darkness of ignorance, hatred, and the numerous negative mindsets that afflict a large percentage of our population.

John 1:5 states that "And the light shines in darkness; and the darkness cannot overcome it!"

And again, in John 8:12, Jesus said, "I am the light of the world: he that followeth me shall not walk in darkness, but shall have the light of life."

The concept of light dispelling darkness is true in the literal and figurative sense, as demonstrated in the "St. Francis Prayer."

> *Lord, make me an instrument of your peace:*
> *Where there is hatred, let me sow love;*
> *Where there is injury, pardon;*
> *Where there is doubt, faith;*
> *Where there is despair, hope;*
> *Where there is darkness, light;*
> *Where there is sadness, joy.*

Hatred cannot exist in the presence of love, so let us love those who profess hate. The Syrian novelist, Nihad Sirees, wrote in his novel, *The Silence and the Roar*, "I believe that love and peace are the right way to confront tyranny." Sirees noted that love and peace can dispel the darkness of oppressive and cruel leadership.

In addition, hatred is harmful to our bodies, whereas love produces feelings of peace and calm. We can achieve more when we entertain feelings of love because our energy is not wasted on hating the people who have harmed us.

Similarly, we can replace the feelings of injury with pardon and forgiveness. The benefits of forgiveness were discussed in another meditation, and it is sufficient to say that when we forgive those that hurt us, the pain of injury will dissipate so that our light can shine. Jesus demonstrated this even as he was dying on the cross, when he said, "Forgive them, for they know not what they do."

Doubt cannot exist in the presence of faith. The *Bhagavad Gita*[6] describes faith as a spiritual journey: "It involves having faith in the divine, surrendering to the higher plan, acting with dedication and detachment, and having faith in the eternal nature of the self."

St. Augustine[7] said, "Faith is to believe what we do not see, and the reward of faith is to see what we believe." I interpret this to mean that if our faith is strong enough, we will work fearlessly to achieve our dreams, and whatever we believe will come to pass.

Setbacks cannot discourage a man who pursues his goal with a single-mindedness powered by the strong flame of faith. There is absolutely no space for doubt in

---

[6] Hindu Scripture dated back to 1st century BCE
[7] 354-430 renowned theologian, prolific writer, skilled preacher.

a heart brimmed with faith.

Linked to the concept of faith is hope, which will dispel any feelings of despair. Let us foster hope by our words and by our actions wherever there is despair. The Koran urges us in 3:139, "Do not lose hope nor be sad."

Our thoughts, our actions and the chemistry of our bodies mirror our thoughts of despair of hope. Despair suggests a state of pessimism, mournfulness and inactivity, whereas hope indicates that the holder is optimistic, and is envisioning the successful conclusion of any issue or project. Hope does not require more effort than despair, but is more likely to lead to a more productive life.

A person can entertain hope even in the direst of circumstances. Elie Wiesel, the author of *Night*, a Holocaust survivor and Nobel Peace Prize winner, wrote about her experience in the concentration camp, "Because I remember, I despair. Because I remember, I have the duty to reject despair."

Just as darkness cannot exist in the presence of light, ignorance cannot exist in the presence of knowledge. If we spread the truth and enlighten those with whom we come in contact, ignorance will evaporate like vapor in the sunlight. In addition to knowing about the outside world, knowledge and clarity about oneself is crucial. Deepak Chopra defines "clarity" as "the state of seeing clearly," and explains, "As you begin to view others as mirrors of yourself, it is as if you move into a new reality in which you experience life with astonishing crystal vision. You learn the lesson of clarity in the exact moments that you accomplish this perspective shift."

In this way, you would have shed light to dispel the darkness of ignorance about yourself.

Wherever there is sadness, let us spread joy and happiness, which is our natural state of being. In this context, I am defining happiness as the deep feeling of being at one with the universe, as opposed to happiness which is linked to specific external events in our lives.

Naturally, people are sad when negative events, such as the death of a loved one occur. And they should be allowed a suitable period of grieving, but when sadness pervades their lives for prolonged periods without any ostensible cause, they should receive some form of spiritual counselling. Very often this will involve listening to the sufferers as they talk about their struggles, and offering whatever help is needed on that occasion. Helping people put things in perspective will also prove useful.

Lighting a candle to dispel darkness very often has a snowball effect. Most of us have encountered people who have helped us along the way, who have brought in light into the darkness of our lives. Many people helped me in my struggles. One of the most prominent was Dr. John McInnes, whom I was lucky to meet when I was struggling during my first years in Canada. He was my advisor in my Masters, and Ph.D. programs. He was quite well-off and didn't need anything from me, but I promised him that my students would benefit from the kindness he had shown me.

I have made every effort to keep that promise, and I have asked my students to pass it along and light a candle, instead of cursing the darkness. In this meditation, I am advising my readers to share the light of knowledge, love, understanding, faith and hope with others so that our lives will glow.

40 LOVE YOUR BODY

In her book, *If life is a Game, These are the Rules,* Cherie Carter Scott entitled one the chapters, "You Will Receive A Body." She goes on to say, "The body you are given will be yours for the duration of your time here. Love it, or hate it, accept it or reject it, it is the only one you will receive in this lifetime." Carter-Scott goes on to explain that the relationship between you and your body "is the most fundamental and important relationship of your lifetime."

With regards to respecting your body, Carter-Scott quotes Suzy Prudden, an author and self-help coach, who wrote, "Your body is your vehicle for life. As long as you are here, live in it. Love, honor, respect and cherish it, treat is well, and it will serve you in kind."

It is important to note here that Carter-Scott makes a distinction between the real you and your body. The body houses the real you—your essential spirit and soul—and acts as a buffer between you and the outside world. Unfortunately, many people judge you only by the way your outer body appears. However, it is important to remember that the only judge that matters is you. That's why it is crucial that you should unconditionally accept and love your body.

One poet, Lang Leav[8], explains this concept

---

[8] b1980. New Zealand Poet, novelist author of *Love & Misadventure*

beautifully:

> *Your body is*
> *a work of art,*
> *a testament to strength,*
> *the home of your soul.*

Do you think that your body is too short, too tall, too dark or too fair, or do you accept your body with all its flaws? Oliver Cromwell totally accepted his body when he told the painter whom he had commissioned to paint his portrait, to paint him as he truly was, "warts and all."

Does acceptance mean that you do not engage in transforming your body? For example, should you engage in activities designed to lose weight or to develop more prominent muscles? Absolutely! You can always try to make your body better, but this does not mean that you should not love and respect it as it is.

Most people know what their bodies can tolerate and what their bodies are allergic to. If you know that you are allergic to peanut butter, for instance, would you eat it? Yet many of us know that certain foods and drinks are not good for us, and we still consume them. For example, many alcoholics are aware that they have a strange allergy to alcohol, and that when they start drinking, they cannot stop although they know of the havoc that alcohol is creating within their bodies. Yet they take that first drink and ignore the harm that they are doing to the temples housing their spirits.

Denial of drugs does not mean that you shouldn't do things that bring pleasure to the body. On the contrary, your body loves to be pampered, and you should take time off from your busy schedule and indulge in activities like walking, playing games, having a relaxing massage, or eating a leisurely lunch with friends, instead of over-working and stressing your body. Many people suffer from heart attacks, high blood pressure and other ailments because they don't take the time to relax. It is crucial to make a commitment to love and take care of your body and respect its awesome intelligence and resilience.

Speaking for myself, I shudder when I think of how much I abused my body in the past, and I marvel and thank God that it is still here to serve me. Now, I have decided to respect it, listen to it and learn the lessons it is offering me.

In addition to abusing my body, I harbored a deep void and a yearning to please others and focused on helping others, to the total neglect of my body. After receiving warning signs, I made the commitment to love and take care of my body, because I realise that I can only look after others when I am in good health.

In an aircraft, the steward or stewardess advises passengers that, in the event of an oxygen shortage, masks will drop. Passengers are told that they should put on their own masks first, before putting on the masks of their dependents. The reason is simple. If they lose consciousness, they will not be able to help anybody.

I counselled some of my siblings to look after themselves before helping others. One brother, who is the founder of *New Millenium Ministries* and a pastor in a church in the USA, always acted as if he were superman, and tried to solve his siblings' problems to the neglect of himself. I was concerned for his well-being and had to tell him that if he should suffer from a severe stroke, or if he is dead, he will be of no use to the extended family.

It is important to take care of your loved ones and the planet on which we live. It is also important to strive to improve the human condition of the people who are not as fortunate as we are, and with whom we share this beautiful planet. However, to do this, we have to be able and healthy. So, love your beautiful body and take care of it. It will thank you and serve you well during your stay on earth.

41 CO-OPERATE WITH THE INEVITABLE

Most of us have experienced misfortunes in our lives. The level of peace and success that we have achieved is linked to our co-operation with events over which we had no control. We should make the best of the circumstances in which we find ourselves, instead of expending energy fighting with the inevitable.

Dale Carnegie cites Elsie MacCormick, who wrote in the *Readers Digest* magazine: "When we stop fighting with the inevitable, we release energy which enables us to create a richer life."

Co-operation with the inevitable is linked to the concept of acceptance, but goes further than acceptance because it involves persistence despite negative events, instead of bemoaning them and trying to change the fact that they occurred. Muslims have a word, "kismet," meaning "fate" for events over which we have no control.

Dale Carnegie compared trying to change the inevitable, which includes the past, as "trying to saw sawdust." In *The Great Gatsby,* by F. Scott Fitzgerald, Gatsby's tragic flaw was that he tried to repeat the past, and this misconception led to his demise.

This philosophy is outlined very succinctly in the

"Serenity Prayer," written by Dr. Reinhold Niebuhr[9]:

God grant me the serenity
To accept the things I cannot change,
The courage to change the things I can
And the wisdom to know the difference.

With regard to co-operating with the inevitable, Dale Carnegie, in his book, *How to Stop Worrying and Start living,* devoted an entire chapter to the concept of accepting and co-operating with the inevitable, and gives an example of a man who was operating an elevator in New York. His left hand was cut off at this wrist, and when Carnegie asked him if the loss of his hand bothered him, he replied, "Oh no, I hardly ever think about it...The only time I ever think about it is when I try to thread a needle."

Carnegie quoted William James, the American philosopher, who said, "Be willing to have it so. Acceptance of what has happened is the first step to overcome any misfortune."

Another example given by Carnegie was the situation in which Jack Dempsey, the famous boxer, found himself when he lost the heavyweight championship fight to Gene Tunney in 1926. He had inevitably aged, and was no match for the younger Tunney. When he lost a second time to Tunney the following year, Dempsey decided to co-operate with the inevitability of aging and opened a restaurant which also promoted prize fights. The restaurant was very successful and attracted many

---

[9] 1892-1971 American theologian, ethicist who influenced politicians.

patrons, including those who were interested in boxing.

Tunney demonstrated that we have no control over aging, but we have control over how we react to the fact that we get older.

Many writers who have been incarcerated used the enforced confinement to pen acclaimed books. For example, Dr. Martin Luther King Jr., an advocate for the rights of Black people in the Southern U.S., was jailed many times. He used the periods of incarceration to write several letters advocating civil disobedience and the moral responsibility of people to disobey unjust laws. The compilation of his letters in his book, *Letters From Birmingham Jail* was published in 1963.

Another example is Nelson Mandela, who wrote *Conversations With Myself* during the twenty-seven years he was in prison on Robben Island for challenging the White supremacy rule in South Africa. The book offers insights into the innermost workings of the mind of the great leader.

Perhaps the most stirring example of resilience and acceptance of the inevitable is exemplified in the story of Helen Keller who lost her sight and hearing after an illness at the age of nineteen months. Helen was forced to communicate with signs until the age of seven when she was fortunate to meet Anne Sullivan, who taught her language, including reading and writing .

Undaunted by her disability, Helen went on to attend Radcliffe College of Harvard University, and became the first deaf and blind person to earn a Bachelor of Arts degree. She went on to write 14 books and essays on several topics, including employment opportunities for people with disabilities and issues relating to equity.

Helen also gave numerous speeches.

Co-operating with the inevitable allows us to be in harmony, instead of conflicting with the universe. When we are in sync with the universal power, our bodies, minds and emotions are at peace, and our creative juices are released. We can better serve humanity in this state of co-operation with the inevitable than we can in a state of agitation.

Let us strive, then, to co-operate with the inevitable.

42 DEATH

Try as we might, we cannot avoid death, the great equalizer. Death will inevitably touch the great and the humble, the rich and the poor. The people in power, the haughty and the rich need to be reminded of this when they think that they have nothing in common with the poor and the humble.

Shakespeare and John Fletcher remind us of this when they wrote in the play *The Two Noble Kinsmen*: "This world's a city, full of straying streets; And death's the market-place where we all meet."

Death is inevitable, but we have a choice in how we respond to the reality of death and this will determine how we spend our time on earth.

Death is an end of our lives on earth, but in a sense, we experience a form of death many times during our stay on this planet. For example, when we lose a friendship, it is a form of death, or when we move from one house to another, it is a form of the death of one experience and the beginning of another. And when we grow physically, emotionally and spiritually, it is death of the old self and birth of the new self. This is implied in the Christian belief that when you accept Jesus Christ as your savior, you are born again.

Hindus believe in the concept of reincarnation, or *samsara,* a continuous cycle of death and rebirth until the individual reaches the state of *moksha*, or eternal bliss. Is it possible that we experience a form of reincarnation on earth, that we die and are born again many times during the growth process?

Many writers explore the phenomenon of death.

In Eckhart Tolle's book, *Stillness Speaks,* he devotes an entire chapter to "Death and the Eternal" and observes:

When you walk through a forest that has not been tamed and interfered with by humans, you will see abundant life all around you, but you will also encounter fallen trees and decaying trunks, rotting leaves and decomposing matter at every step. Wherever you look, you will find death as well as life.

Tolle explains that death is necessary for life and observes that numerous forms of organisms thrive on the decaying matter of dead plants and animals.

For those who fear death, Alexander Pope wrote a beautiful poem about death, entitled, *A Dying Christian to his Soul.* Pope's last two lines of the poem, "O Grave! Where is thy victory? / O Death! Where is thy sting?" should give them some courage.

Antiphanes, a Greek writer, advises us to embrace death:

Be not grieved above measure for thy deceased friends. They are not dead, but have only finished the journey which it is necessary for every one of us to take. We ourselves must go to that great place of reception in which all of them are assembled, and in this general rendezvous of mankind, live together in another state of being.

Of course, not all writers accept death so stoically.

Dylan Thomas exhorts us, "Do not go gentle into that good night, / Old age should burn and rave at close of day;/Rage, rage against the dying of the light."

Many religious figures teach that, while our present physical bodies will decompose, our souls will live forever, either in God's presence or be eternally separated from Him, depending on our actions on earth.

Our physical bodies temporarily house our essential spirit, our souls, and when our physical bodies die, the soul does not. It simply leaves our bodies which housed it temporarily, and finds another home. In effect, you are not dead. You have simply "shed your mortal coil."

Whenever I go to a funeral, I am reminded of my own mortality and this makes me determined to live my life on earth in a meaningful manner. The concept of death, for me, is an encouragement to live life fully because I know that the time I spend on earth is not infinite.

We cannot avoid death, so let the certainty of death encourage us to live well and wisely.

43 DEPRESSION

Craig Sawchuck, a clinical psychologist at the Mayo Clinic, describes depression:

Depression is a mood disorder that causes a persistent feeling of sadness and loss of interest. Also called major depressive disorder or clinical depression, it affects how you feel, think and behave and can lead to a variety of emotional and physical problems. You may have trouble doing normal day-to-day activities, and sometimes you may feel as if life isn't worth living.

The Bible shows us that depression can affect anyone. Poor people like Naomi, the mother-in-law of Ruth, and very rich people like King Solomon suffered from depression. Young people like David and older people like Job were also afflicted. Depression can impact a person's health, his relationships, and his ability to survive in this world.

On a physical level, depression is linked to heart disease, increased risk of substance abuse, insomnia, and the weakening of the immune system, leading to various forms of illnesses.

Socially, depression can lead to employment problems, strain on relationships, suicidal thoughts and even attempts at suicide, among other issues.

Many relatives and friends of people who suffer from depression are at a loss with regards to what support they can provide to their loved ones.

Experts from The Mayo Clinic suggest that you urge the person to get medical help, because many forms of depression are caused by a chemical imbalance in the body. Convincing a person who is suffering from depression to see a doctor may require some effort because the sufferer may refuse to acknowledge that he is unwell. You should also ensure that the depressed person takes the medication as prescribed.

A person suffering from depression needs to be convinced that he is not at fault, that he is not experiencing depression alone, and that there is help.

You should also make the time to listen to the person as he tells you how he feels, and should constantly let him know how much he is loved and treasured, and offer any assistance that will make his life less stressful. Remind him of his positive qualities and his significant achievements and let him know that you want to understand how he is feeling.

You should encourage him to join a group involved in an activity which interests him. This will provide him with an opportunity to indulge in something which holds his interest and to interact with like-minded people.

Recovering from depression usually takes time, so it is important to remind the person suffering from depression to be patient. it is also important for you to be patient with yourself, as you watch your loved one slowly recovering.

Meditation and affirmations are useful in coping with depression and are frequently used in combination with medications. In our meditations, we can remind ourselves often that the world is a friendly place and that we, as children of God, deserve peace, love and happiness. We can develop affirmations such as, "I am filled with love, peace and forgiveness of myself and others for errors of the past." When affirmations are repeated frequently, they become part of your thinking. I can tell you that affirmations work, because I've used them successfully in my battle with anxiety. You can tailor your affirmations to fit your specific situation.

If you are suffering from depression, it is important that you know that there is hope, and that others who have faced this debilitating illness have survived and sometimes even thrived. For example, J.K. Rowling, the author who created Harry Potter, got married in Portugal and gave birth to a daughter. After her marriage broke down, she returned to Scotland and was forced to accept government handouts. Rowling began to suffer from depression and even contemplated suicide as she was writing *Harry Potter*. Her novel was rejected by several publishers, until it was finally accepted by a small publication house, Bloomsbury, in London and became a best seller. Rowling is now a billionaire, and at the time of my writing, is the world's richest novelist.

Not all of us can be successful as Rowling. The example of another author, Matt Haig, is not as dramatic but just as compelling. Haig overcame his depression by appreciating all the "little things" around him that made his life worthwhile. In his book, *Reasons to Stay Alive* he describes his struggles with depression and the process by which he engaged in reading and writing, together with focusing on his love for his parents and girlfriend to overcome depression.

Haig's lesson is for us to notice and appreciate the little things in life—a beautiful sunset, a flower, and the human relationships that we previously took for granted and neglected to appreciate.

It is also crucial that we eat well, get enough exercise, and that we do not abuse our bodies by ingesting harmful substances. Many people are familiar with the Latin phrase, *Mens sana in corpore sano,* which means, *A sound mind in a sound body.* When you exercise, the body produces endorphins—a feel-good chemical—which gives you a natural high and helps you cope with negative thinking and the ensuing negative feeling. I know that this is true because I've jogged for most of my life, not so much for the physical benefits, but because it made me emotionally stable.

Depression can be conquered if we take the medications prescribed by our medical practitioners, work hard in maintaining our mental health, and in keeping our bodies fit. As children of the universe, we should expect and accept the abundant love that the universe has to offer and rejoice in it.

Depression will have no place in a world full of love, abundance and caring.

44 KNOW WHAT WORKS FOR YOU

Many people strive to understand the world and the devices we use in our daily lives. I had a brother, for example, who would take apart clocks, radios and other devices to learn how they work. However, although it is crucial that we learn about ourselves, few people take the trouble to discover what works for them.

Pythagoras is reputed to have said, "Man, know thyself; then thou shalt know the universe and God."

It is important that you know what works for you, physically, mentally, emotionally and spiritually. You should certainly seek the counsel of other people and act on the advice that you think best, but it is essential that you follow your own moral compass, and not let random criticism dissuade you from doing what is right, and what is best for you.

One of Aesop's fables illustrates this beautifully:

A man and his son were going to the market with their donkey. The man decided to ride the donkey and have his son walk by his side. As he passed a group of people, one of the men in the group said, "Look at that selfish man. He is riding the donkey, and has his son walking."

So, the man jumped off the donkey, put his son on the donkey's back, and walked beside his son and the donkey. Before long, they passed another group of people, and one of them said, "Look at that foolish man. He is letting his young son, who is full of energy, ride the donkey and he is walking."

Confused, the man jumped on the donkey's back with his son, and when they passed another group of people, one of them observed, "Look at that selfish man and his son, both of them riding the poor donkey."

Not knowing what to do, the man jumped off the donkey, took his son off the donkey and they both walked beside the animal. They had not gone more than five hundred yards before they came to another group of people. "Look at that stupid man," one of them said. "They have that donkey, and both of them are walking."

The poor confused and frustrated man, not knowing what to do, lifted the donkey on his shoulders, and with his son beside him, walked to the market.

Needless to say, the man should have done what worked for him and his son, instead of adjusting his actions every time somebody criticized him.

Tell people that you have a minor illness, and you will have multiple suggestions for remedies, each person telling you that his or her remedy is sure to work. That remedy most likely worked for them, but there is no guarantee that it will work for you because each person is different. For example, my wife drinks coconut water because it contains potassium which her doctor told her that her body needs. I have been cautioned not to drink coconut water, because it has potassium and the medication which my doctor had previously prescribed for me causes my body to produce potassium. Drinking coconut water works for her, and not for me.

In everyday matters, each person will give advice based on his experiences and on his concept of the world.

However, not everyone has the same world view, and it would be inadvisable for you follow the advice of someone whose world view differs from your own. For example, there are people who believe that the world exists for their benefit, and there are people, including prominent politicians, who are suffering from a delusion that they are the center of the universe. Such people may advise and encourage you to take advantage of someone's misfortunes. However, your world view may be that we live in a world where we cooperate with instead of competing, and you may want to lend a helping hand to a person in need.

As far as mental activities are concerned, nobody can tell you how best you can learn. We all have different learning styles, and we know when and how we best engage in intellectual activities. For example, I learn best in the morning. My son, on the other hand, struggles to keep his eyes open in the mornings, and by the evening when I am tired, he is fully awake and ready to pick up his books.

As far as learning styles are concerned, it is important for you to know and accept unconditionally that you are a unique human being with your distinctive learning style, of which you should be proud. The best teachers adopt a variety of teaching methods which cater to the different learning styles of their students. As lifelong students on this planet, it is important that we know and acknowledge how we learn best, and the times when we are at our peak intellectually.

For example, I belong to a writing group, and one of the members shared that he wrote best at 2:30 in the morning "when his creative juices are flowing." On the other hand, the author of *The Kite Runner,* Khaled Hosseini, found that he wrote best at 5:00 a.m. No author should blindly follow the writing styles and habits of other writers, but should know himself and write in a style he is comfortable in and at a time that works best for him. Many people have positively commented on the simplicity of my writing style. I am comfortable with using very simple language in my writing and I will continue to write in this style.

We are all also unique emotionally, and react differently to different stimuli. For example, people respond differently to stress. Caroline Mazure, a professor in Women's Health Research, advises that, when faced with a stressful situation, "It's helpful to find the methods of relaxation and self-care **that work best for you.**" [Author's emphasis]

Some people relax when they are involved in a specific type of exercise. I discovered that jogging worked best for me in my struggle to cope with anxiety, and jogged for many years to keep my body and mind in good shape. If exercise is the outlet best for you, choose the form of exercise that best meets your needs. Some people find that Yoga or Tai Chi relaxes them. Others may find that meditation, or a combination of exercise and meditation works best for them. You can discover what method works best for you by trial and error.

When you get involved in physical activities, know what you can do physically, and be guided by this knowledge. Don't worry about who can run faster than you, or who can lift more weights than you. Exercise at a time when it's best for you, and do the type and amount of exercise that meets your needs. Remember the lines from *Desiderata:* "If you compare yourself with others,/You may become vain and bitter/ For always there will be greater and lesser persons than yourself."

You also know what triggers you emotionally, and can avoid topics that elicit negative emotions. For example, my wife and I are aware that we always respond negatively to certain topics, and that broaching those topics almost certainly result in quarrels. We make sure that we avoid those topics. Avoidance is an action, and in this instance, avoidance works for us.

It is crucial that you find your spiritual centre, and it is also important for you to know that you are not the centre of the universe—that there is a power greater than yourself. Some people call this power God, or Allah, or Brahman, or simply My Higher Power. Whatever you choose to call this power greater than yourself, you should strive to know the *Will* of this power. Then act in accordance with that *Will* of *your* Higher Power.

Strive to know yourself, do what works for you in all dimensions of your life, and be at peace with yourself and the universe.

45 EGO VS SELF

If you ask yourself, "Who am I?" the answer is likely to be, "I am a teacher, a farmer," or whatever profession in which you are engaged.

But are you *the job* in which you are occupied at the present time? Perhaps you are a father or a mother, the owner of a house or a car. You may be fulfilling all the above roles, along with numerous roles not listed above, but they are not you.

Who, then, are you? Deep within the person fulfilling all the roles in the objective world is your innermost being. Philosophers call this innermost being by various names. Deepak Chopra, in his book *The Seven Spiritual Laws of Success,* calls it "...your true Self, which is your spirit, your soul...It is immune to criticism, it is unfearful of any challenge, and it feels beneath no one. And yet it is humble and feels superior to no one, because it recognizes that everyone else is the same *Self,* the same spirit in different disguises."

What then, is this spirit? Close your eyes for a few seconds and feel the energy field in your body flowing from head to toe, from toe to head. This is the energy that keeps your body alive and is your true self, or your soul, or spirit.

The energy field that you feel in your body is the same energy field that is within other humans and all living things, because we are a localized body of energy in a world of energy. This energy creates a bond between us and the rest of the world. If you are part of the energy field that is all around you, how can you be separate from the rest of the world?

On the wall of the office of one of my friends is a page:

NAMASTE
My soul honors your soul.
I honor the place in you where the entire universe resides.
I honor the light, love, truth, beauty and peace within you,
Because it is also within me.
In sharing these things, we are united, we are the same.
We are one.

What then, is the *ego*? The ego is our sense of self-importance and separateness. It is our belief that we are our personality, talents, and abilities, and is in constant competition with other egos for material gains, for recognition, or for any rewards that make us attain ascendancy over others.

Chopra tells us, "The ego, however, is not who you really are. The ego is your self-image; it is your social mask; it is the role you are playing. Your social mask thrives on approval. It wants to control, and it is sustained by power, because it lives in fear."

The most fundamental error most people make is mistaking the *ego* for the *self*. Eckhart Tolle, the author of, *The Power of Now,* tells us that the ego is the false sense of self, and explains that the ego, like all living things and mechanisms wants to survive, and will create all kinds of drama in our relationship with others and with our environment to survive.

We have spent years building our egos, living inside them, and reinforcing them, and this makes it difficult to recognise our genuine selves. To be at one with yourself, learn to recognize when you are smitten with the sense of self-importance, and go deeply within yourself, feel the energy field within your body, and recognise that this energy or spirit is the real you. Don't be discouraged if you cannot feel this energy field strongly when you first attempt to go deeply within your body. As you repeatedly practice this exercise, you will feel your life's energy stronger and stronger. It has always been there, and with practice you will be able to focus your attention more on it.

Eventually, you will gradually realise that you are sharing the same energy field with all living things. This feeling of sharing will slowly overshadow the ego, and strengthen the sense of self.

I have been strengthening my ego and have lived in a world of competition for most of my life. This meant that I was rarely at peace with myself. Yes, I have experienced moments of happiness when I passed an important examination, or achieved something significant, but that happiness was short-lived, and I resorted to spending my time and energy in trying to achieve more.

Now, I take some time every day to go within my body and feel the localized energy field within me. Then I attempt to merge this energy field with the universal energy field, and feel at one with the universe and all living things within it. I can experience this state of bliss for only a few seconds, although Yogis are able to do this for long periods of time. However, I am cognisant of the fact that knowing I am part of a larger universe is important. I am also patient about my progress and I am satisfied with feeling this "oneness with the universe" for brief periods at a time. I aim for progress, not perfection in detaching myself from the ego and strengthening my *true self*. For the short while that I experience the merging of my local energy with the universal energy, I am suffused with a feeling of peace, and I am truly grateful to have discovered my true self, if only for brief periods.

You, too, can experience these moments of bliss if you make a conscious decision to strengthen your sense of self, instead of feeding the ego. The feeling of peace and harmony with the universe is well worth the effort.

46 YOU'RE ONLY HUMAN

There are so many people who hold positions of power or responsibility that they forget the fact that they are only human. The Quran reminds us that we are on this earth for a short while: "When their specified time arrives, they cannot delay it for a single hour nor can they bring it forward." (Quran, 16:61)

And Genesis, chapter 3, verse 19 tells us, "Dust thou art, and unto dust shalt thou return."

We should constantly remind ourselves and others of this simple truth, regardless of how much power or influence we have. For example, Marcus Aurelius, an emperor of Rome was so concerned that he might let his power go to his head that he instructed his servant to whisper in his ear, "You're just a man. You're just a man," every time a citizen bowed to him, called out a word of praise, or when crowds cheered him.

However, not everybody was as wise as Marcus Aurelius. Percy Blythe Shelley wrote an enlightening poem describing a pedestal that a traveller encountered. The last six lines of the poem reads thus:

"Ozymandias"

And on the pedestal, these words appear:
"My name is Ozymandias, King of Kings;
Look on my Works, ye Mighty and despair!"
Nothing beside remains. Round the decay
Of that colossal Wreck, boundless and bare

The lonely and level sands stretch far away.

This is a reminder that regardless of how much power and money that we have, we all will succumb to death. In the case of Ozymandias, even the statue he had built to commemorate his power and success crumbled.

All the kings and queens, all the billionaires, all the moguls eventually die, because they are human.

The next time a person who is wealthy or a person who has a great deal of power tells you that you have nothing in common, remind him that you do have at least one thing in common. In ten years, or twenty, or sixty, you both will be lifeless corpses, and then ashes, or piles of dust, or mummified.

We may think that we are important, that we have money or influence, but the truth is that we are minor specks in the universe of time and space, especially when we view the length of our lifespans in perspective. Shakespeare reminded us of this in his tragedy, *Macbeth*. When Macbeth learns of his wife's death, he says:

...Out, out, brief candle! Life's but a walking shadow, a poor player
That struts and frets his hour upon the stage
And then is heard no more: it is a tale
Told by an idiot, full of sound and fury,
Signifying nothing...(Act 5, Scene 5)

The awareness that you're only human can be useful at another level. Whenever you aim for perfection and fail, you need to remind yourself of your humanity. Whenever you feel depressed, angry, sad, or you experience negative emotions, you need to remind yourself that you're only human and forgive yourself.

Billy Joel, a prominent singer, was wrestling with depression and thoughts of suicide. He shared with reporters that he wrote the song, "You're Only Human (Second Wind)" to help people who were suffering from these debilitating emotional illnesses. His song, including the verse quoted below, reminds listeners to accept their humanity:

You're having a hard time and lately you don't feel so good
You're getting a bad reputation in your neighborhood
(It's all right), it's all right sometimes that's what it takes
You're only human, you're allowed to make your share of mistakes.
(Only human, ooh-ooh)

Another level at which we should accept our humanity is to accept our bodies and our body functions completely, instead of being ashamed of them. Remember you are only human. We need to recognize the fact that kings and queens, commoners, the rich and the poor are as human as we are, and have the same body functions.

When we are awed by those who possess power, wealth and privilege, we need to remind ourselves of this fact. Pierre Trudeau, a former Prime Minister of Canada, was with an aide when some members of the royal family visited Canada from England. When the aide stood by his side open-mouthed and dumbstruck as he admired the visiting royals who were dressed in all their finery, Trudeau simply reminded him, "Remember they shit too."

How does this awareness of our own humanity, the humanity of others, and the certainty of death lead us to live better lives? When we have accepted the fact that we and others with whom we are sharing this beautiful planet are just "passing through," we will treat ourselves and all with whom we come in contact with reverence and respect, so that we will leave some pleasant memories for others when our physical bodies have dissolved.

Let us accept our humanity and the humanity of others with whom we share this beautiful planet.

47 KARMA

Most people know karma as "What you sow you will reap" or "What goes around must come around." The principle is that whatever we do will come back to us, and this is the motivation to do good to others so that positive things will happen in our lives.

Deepak Chopra, in his book, *The Seven Spiritual Laws of Success,* devotes an entire chapter to karma, or cause and effect. He explains the law of karma as: "Every action generates a force of energy that returns to us in kind...what we sow is what we reap. And when we choose actions that bring happiness and success to others, the fruit of our karma is happiness and success." Later in the chapter, Chopra emphasizes, "... the law of Karma says that no debt in the universe goes unpaid."

One yogi, Swami Vivekananda, explains karma very succinctly: "Our thoughts, words and deeds are the threads of the net which we throw around ourselves."

Many people focus only on deeds when they think of karma, but it is important to note that Vivekananda includes thoughts and words along with deeds. In *Soul Krave,* a website exploring the psychology of humans, one researcher wrote, "The power of thought is truly amazing. Every time you entertain an idea or contemplate a belief, you emit a distinctive electromagnetism. In other words, your personal vibration changes. And this vibration isn't just important to your mood and your success—it influences everything around you as well. The truth is that everything is energy!"

You've most likely heard someone say something like, "Joan has an aura of peace around her," or "Tom has an aura of negativity." The thoughts of people create a kind of energy around them which others can feel. This influences not only the persons entertaining the thoughts, but also the thoughts and actions of people around them. Needless to say, people would prefer to be around others who emit positive auras rather than negative ones.

When you think harmful thoughts about anyone, you create negative energy which ultimately comes back to you. That is why you should forgive those who hurt you. You do this not for them but for yourself, because when you harbour feelings of anger and hate, it does a great deal of harm to your body without hurting the other person.

As far as words are concerned, we all heard the saying, "Sticks and stones may break my bones, but words will never hurt me."

This is erroneous, because words can hurt us even more that sticks and stones. Words have played a great part in shaping our lives, and many people bear emotional scars from something hurtful that somebody said to them. For example, one friend and I were serving on a committee relating to anti-racist education. My friend, who is Black, told the group, "I don't think any of you can imagine how hurtful it feels when somebody calls you the *N* word."

Words can also have a self-fulfilling prophecy. If a

person hears that he will amount to nothing, it's possible he will think it is futiile to strive to achieve, and may settle for less than he is capable of.

Chopra says that the key factor about karma is the conscious choice making, in which we are involved numerous times a day. For example, we are conditioned to be offended when someone insults us, and to be pleased when someone flatters us. Pavlov demonstrated such conditioning when he rang a bell just before his dog was given food. After a while, the dog salivated whenever he heard the bell, even when no food was available.

Can you think of a situation in which a person might not be offended when someone insults him or her, but instead either examines his or her own behavior and tries to determine whether the insult is justified? Can you imagine a situation in which even if the insult is not justified, the person feels compassion for the person who is offensive, and is aware that the person who insulted him unjustly must be really hurting to act in this manner?

It is possible to respond to an unjustified insult with love. For example, a prominent politician, Jagmeet Singh, a Sikh who wears a turban, was speaking at a meeting when a woman who thought that he was a Muslim, insulted him and called him a terrorist.

Singh could have responded in several ways. He could have pointed out to her that he was not a Muslim. He could have emphasized that not all Muslims are terrorists. He could have traded insults and called her ignorant.

Instead, he made the choice to tell her, "We all love

you! Know that we all love you."

By showering her with love, he disarmed her and calmed the people who attended the meeting, which progressed peacefully after the incident.

Chopra says, "When you make a choice... you can ask yourself two things. First, what are the consequences of this choice that I'm making? Secondly, will this choice that I'm making bring happiness to me and to those around me?" If your body sends a message of comfort, then it is the right choice. If it sends a message of discomfort, then you should re-think the choice.

We have no control of the past, but we can make the correct choices now and in the future, thereby creating good karma for ourselves.

The Website *WebMD, Health and Balance Resource,* offers some suggestions for the creation of good karma:

- *Do everything with kindness, and show kindness to everyone around you. When you move with kindness, you attract positive karma that encourages everyone and everything to be kind to you.*
- *Chant a mantra with positive thoughts of others in mind. It helps clear away any negative karma you're carrying around you.*
- *Meditate. When you meditate, try to clear your mind and think about why you are meditating. Meditate, feeling grateful for your life and where you are right now.*
- *Be gracious in both wins and losses. Generously celebrate other people's wins and successes and humbly accept your failures. You'll attract good*

karma for the future and receive grace and generosity from others whether you're doing well or not.

- *Give to charity. Giving helps you attract good karma because it brings generosity from others to you when you need it.*
- *Be there for others, even when it's inconvenient. Being there for people needing a listening ear or support, even strangers, helps you cultivate kindness and attracts good karma. Someone will be there for you when you need support.*
- *Appreciate the life of all beings, especially the tiniest of creatures. You'll attract the karma of a long life by doing so.*

But what about past karma?

Chopra emphasizes that we have to pay our karmic debts, even if it involves a great deal of pain. We must make amends to those whom we have hurt, and seek their forgiveness. Making amends is not an act of weakness, but of strength.

Another way is to transform your karma into a more desirable experience. Learn from your mistakes and use your learning to help others. One way I am trying to use my learning from past mistakes is by sharing my thoughts in this book which I hope will help some people live better lives.

The third way to deal with past karma is through deep meditation, in which you go into what Chopra calls *the gap,* the place of no mind and experience the *Self,* the *Spirit.* You wash or transcend the seeds of your karma by going into the gap, and coming out again. Chopra says that going into the *gap* is like washing dirty clothes. Every time you go into the *gap*, the clothes come out a bit cleaner.

Your life on earth is a karmic experience, and you can choose to make it a good one or a negative one. Even though I may not know all my readers, we share the same spirit, and I wish you good karma.

48 TRUST

A prominent anthropologist, Dr. Harry Persaud, informed me that humans had always lived in communities, and that one of the main reasons for their survival was that they trusted each other to protect the community. He indicated that trust has always been one of the mainstays of society, and is the glue that holds human beings together.

Whether we live alone or with others, we need to interact with other people and this involves a degree of trust in the people around us. This includes the professionals whom we trust to take care of our health, welfare and security.

For example, when a person confesses his sins to a priest, he trusts the priest not to publicize them to the remainder of the congregation. We trust our doctors and health professionals and take the medications they prescribe without question—for most of the time anyway. We trust our dentists to place a drill in our mouths, after allowing them to put a long syringe filled with Novocain into our gums. When we travel on an aircraft, we trust the pilot to take us safely to our destination.

The Canadian law, and I suspect the laws of many other countries, recognize that a violation of this trust is a serious offence and has a special term for it. "Breach of Trust" is an offence under Section 122 of the *Criminal Code of Canada,* and applies to public officers who intentionally and knowingly violate the duties of their office or position of trust, with the purpose of gaining personal benefit or causing harm to others. The penalty for this offence can be imprisonment for up to fourteen years.

Some time ago, I challenged the decision of a very prominent university based on trust, and I gave the example of the danger it would cause if mechanics were to change the mechanism of vehicles. I explained that when we get in our vehicles, we trust the manufacturers and feel confident that when we press the brakes the vehicle will stop instead of accelerating. If the manufacturers change the mechanism of vehicles to make them accelerate when the brake pedal is pressed, drivers will become very disoriented and the result will be chaos.

I pointed out that the university had quite clearly specified the system of calculating students' grades in its calendar, but subsequently sent out a brochure by mail which explained that it had changed the system. I argued that students at the university trusted the organization to outline all the rules and procedures in the calendar of that year, and that it was a betrayal of trust and a violation of the by-laws of the university to distribute a brochure contradicting the rules and regulations outlined in the calendar. I asked the Appeal Board to imagine students walking around the university with calendars in their hands, and wondering which rules and procedures were contradicted by mailed brochures. The Appeal Board agreed with me, and the system outlined in the calendar for the calculation of grades was upheld.

There must be a degree of trust in the people in the

community in which we live. In the rustic village where I was born, people sometimes borrowed money or other valuables from each other. As far as I can remember, there were no contracts or documents of any kind, and the only record of the transaction was the borrower's promise to repay the money, or return the valuable. Most people kept their promises, and the odd person who did not do so was known to the villagers as someone who could not be trusted.

When we drive on public roads, we trust the other drivers to observe the laws governing the use of the road and they trust us to do the same. For example, when we drive on a narrow mountain road with a thin line in the middle of the road, we trust other drivers to drive on the right-hand side of the road (in North America) and we hear of horrible accidents that happen when people don't follow the rules of the road.

It is also crucial that we reflect on our own actions and thoughts, because in order for people to have confidence in us, we must be able to believe in ourselves.

In Shakespeare's *Hamlet,* Polonius advises his son, Laertes, as he leaves for university: "This above all: to thine own self be true/ And it must follow, as the night the day/ Thou canst not then be false to any man." Here, Laertes is urged to trust himself.

It takes a long time to build trust, but you can lose it in an instant, as the following anecdote illustrates. I started teaching in a school where some students had an innate distrust of authority, and many of them had run-ins with the law. I reached out to one of these students, who was known to the police and who was living in a group home. Trying to bond with him, I visited the group home where he lived and he proudly showed me his two gerbils, which became the focal point of our future conversations. Gradually, he began to trust me and we developed a rapport, until one day I went to school tired and fighting a cold. In class, the student answered a question incorrectly and I snapped at him.

"You're just like all the rest of them," he told me, as he retreated into himself. Try as I might, I never regained his trust, and that student left me with an important lesson.

Of course, we will sometimes fail in gaining and maintaining the trust of others and of ourselves, but it is important to remind ourselves that despite all the times we failed, we should trust ourselves to continue trying to do the right thing. An anonymous writer wrote, "Self-trust means consistently staying true to yourself. You treat yourself with love and compassion, rather than strive for perfection. You know, deep down, that you can survive difficulties and you refuse to give up on yourself."

In her book, *IF LIFE is A GAME, THESE are the RULES,* Cherie Carter-Scott observes that "You learn the lesson of trust when you take a leap of faith and believe that you inner knowing is guiding you toward a greater good. Trust is the attainment of your instincts to know who and what is in your best interest..."

Carter-Scott cites the example of Emily who has been told what to do, and what not to do throughout her life. When she was thirty-two, Emily wanted to start a business which involved marketing her doll-making kits through mail. She was convinced that her business would be a success because she liked to sew, and had made several doll-making kits for her friends, but her family and friends had advised her against taking the risk. Emily consulted with Carter-Scott who asked her, "Putting aside the practical considerations, and without regard for the outcome, if you could do anything in the world, what would it be?"

"Make my doll-making kits and sell them," Emily replied.

At the encouragement of the Carter-Scott, Emily started her business of making and selling doll-making kits, which was a huge success. Perhaps you know a person who trusted his instincts and succeeded in business, in relationships or in whatever field that held his passion.

We all have an internal compass guiding us along the right path and distinguishing it from the wrong one. Let us trust that compass and move towards the right route.

Imagine what our world would be like if we all can completely trust ourselves and each other!

49 LAUGHTER AS THERAPY

One of the sections of the *Reader's Digest* magazine is entitled "Laughter is the best medicine." It may well be right because many medical practitioners emphasize that laughter benefits our bodies and minds in many ways and urge us to laugh more.

Some of the benefits of laughter are that it:

1. Reduces the level of stress hormones, while increasing the level of health-enhancing hormones.

2. Gives the body a nice internal workout. A good belly laugh exercises the diaphragm, contracts the abdominal muscles and even works out the muscles in the shoulders. It also provides a good workout for the heart.

3. Gives you physical release. Have you ever felt like you had to laugh or you'd cry? Have you experienced the cleansed feeling after a good laugh?

4. Promotes a positive frame of mind and shifts the focus away from negative emotions, making you more cheerful and putting you in a positive frame of mind.

5. Changes your perspective. Researchers found that our response to stressful events can be altered, depending on whether we view something as a "threat" or a "challenge." Humor gives us a more light-hearted perspective and helps us view events as "challenges," thereby making them less threatening and more positive.

6. Lightens the mood of others. Laughter is contagious, so if you bring more laughter into your life, you can most likely help others around you laugh more.

People who laugh a lot and are optimistic have stronger immune systems and can fight off illness better than pessimists.

Linked to the above point, laughter makes you live longer. According to recent research published in the *Archives of General Psychiatry*, optimists live longer than pessimists.

Whether we see a particular incident as funny, or we become upset by it depends on our mindset. Here are some suggestions to increase laughter in your lives:

Try to find the humor in situations. For example: a few years ago, I was driving home from New York where I was attending a book fair. Unfortunately, my elder brother had passed away while I was driving home, and I found my wife very upset when I arrived. Apparently, a family friend had called her, and told her that he heard that I was dead, thus causing her imagination to run rampant. I told her that she should have told him that she spoke with me only a few hours before, and that I sounded quite lucid for a dead man.

You can watch funny movies, and read books that make you laugh. Most of us look at TV anyhow—instead of seeing news or shows that make you sad, watch funny movies that make you laugh. The same goes for books. There are many light-hearted books in the library and bookstores which make you laugh. I must confess that I wrote some of them.

You can make laughter a part of your everyday life by laughing with those close to you. A friend of mine told me that he and his wife go to bed laughing, and wake up laughing. I am not there yet, but I do find occasions to laugh. Indeed, some of my friends say that I frequently overdo it. On the other hand, *Reader's Digest* published one of my jokes.

Try to be around people who have a sense of humor, instead of people who promote doom and gloom. A word of caution though. In encouraging yourself and others to laugh, you must guard against making jokes at other people's expense, because words can hurt.

To my mind, the best humorists laugh at themselves. We all make mistakes, and it is an art to laugh at yourself and invite others to laugh at your mistakes.

Laughter is so beneficial that somebody invented *Laughing Yoga*. I once attended a social gathering at a friend who was enrolled in in one of those classes. She had us all on the floor laughing for laughter's sake. It felt good, and made a positive influence for the remainder of the evening. Even as I'm writing about it, I vividly remember that event, and I feel good about it.

Laughter is really the best medicine and it does not cost you anything. If you want to live a longer, happier and healthier life, laugh. People would like to be around you, and most likely will transfer their joy to others, making your corner of the world a happier place.

50 FREEDOM

When most people talk about freedom, they talk about physical freedom and neglect intellectual, economic and emotional freedom. In this passage, I will focus on emotional, intellectual and economic, freedom, with the understanding that these freedoms are connected to physical slavery. That is why many slave-owners made it illegal for slaves to learn to read and write.

Although physical slavery was made illegal some time ago, how many of us are really free? How many of us have been able to break out of the limiting conditioning to which we were subjected as children. It is true that some of this conditioning was to keep us safe, but the truth is that a great deal of it was consciously or unconsciously designed to maintain the status quo of those in authority.

Very often, the conditioning we received influenced our thinking and behavior throughout our adulthood, and the choices we make are largely determined by it.

Emotional freedom is very hard to achieve, and many of us are emotionally dependent. Do you consistently crave love and attention in general, or from particular persons? I know that I have a need to please, and to feel valued. This emotional need has been recognized by people who have taken advantage of it and manipulated me. Being aware of this need is the first step towards emotional freedom.

With regard to intellectual freedom, the well-known writer and critic, Paulo Freire in his book *Pedagogy of the Oppressed*, claims that schools act as conditioning agents, and therefore limit our intellectual freedom because we are told what to believe. How can we be intellectually free if we are taught materials that are meant to keep us in intellectual cages?

For example, students are taught history predominantly from a Eurocentric perspective. As a young adult, I read of how Columbus discovered America. Now many people are beginning to question this. For example, one of my Grade 12 students in Toronto observed in her presentation to the class, "How can Columbus discover a land with people in it? Were the Native peoples just sitting around fishing and waiting to be discovered by Columbus?"

In Canadian history, the contribution of the Chinese in the construction of the transnational railway, and the numerous injustices they experience have only recently been recognized. And the injustices perpetuated by the Canadian government against Canadian citizens of Japanese ancestry have been largely ignored. Fortunately, "Redress Education," which relates to the above injustices is now being taught in schools.

To prove how many people blindly accept what they have been taught, one teacher of Japanese ancestry called me at the East York Board of Education when I was the anti-racist consultant and complained about a teacher who was teaching the history of the displacement of Japanese Canadians during the war. This unit was recently added to the curriculum, and the teacher who complained was quite comfortable with the old curriculum which omitted this aspect of history.

"Let bygones be bygones," he told me. "Miss Smith (not her real name) is opening old wounds by teaching children all the hardships our ancestors suffered at the hands of Canadians. We don't need to open old wounds."

"We have to teach students about the past, and how it affects the present," I told him. Then I quoted George Santayana who said, "Those who cannot remember the past are condemned to repeat it."

The complainer persisted and I had to meet with him and explain that it is crucial that students be made aware of history, even if it is unpleasant, in order that future generations can guard against making the same mistakes. I explained that if we refrain from teaching about the Holocaust, for example, because we do not want "to open old wounds," we would be doing students a great injustice.

The complainant reluctantly acquiesced.

Economic freedom is something we are striving for. We all have our bills to pay. We all have to eat, and we all need money for incidental expenses. Most of us have enough to live, but how many of us can say that we have economic freedom? How many of us are tied to jobs we do not like because it pays the bills? The benefits of doing a job that we really want to do are discussed in another meditation.

The good news is that we can recognize our past conditioning and we can break out of it. When we do this, we are able to question ideas that were previously held to be indisputable facts.

To have a critical mind does not mean you have to be confrontational, because it can all happen inside your head. When you begin to do this, there will be an awakening within you that will be the light of freedom. This light will become brighter, and while it may be difficult to break completely from a lifetime of conditioning, you will begin to experience what Jesus meant when he said, "You shall know the truth, and the truth shall set you free."

51 GENEROSITY

Generosity is one the most admired traits of humans who have lived in communities for several reasons. One of these is that members could help those in need in a number of ways—if they are injured, if they need food or any material items necessary for survival, or if they need physical, mental or emotional support. This, of course, means that members of the community have to be generous with material things or with their time and expertise.

For example, in the rural community where I was born and raised, some people were good at building; some were skilled in the use of herbal remedies, and some had mechanical skills. Of course, payment was given to some technicians for extensive work such as building a house, but mostly people were generous with their time and expertise.

Deepak Chopra says this about generosity: "If you ask people why they give, the readiest answers offer clues to the mystery. God wants me to. I feel better about myself. Others need, and I have. I want to share. It's only right."

Hebrews 13:16 tells us, "Generosity is a simple act. And do not forget to do good and to share with others, for with such sacrifices God is pleased."

And Acts 20:35 says, "I have shown you in every way, by laboring like this, that you must support the weak. And remember the words of the Lord Jesus, *It is more blessed to give than to receive.*"

Author Christian Smith wrote in the magazine, *Science of Generosity:*

> *Why are people generous? Why are some humans much more generous than others? What factors tend to promote or inhibit generosity? It turns out that generosity makes a big difference in the quality of human personal and social life, both for the givers and receivers. So the better we understand it, the better we will be able to think about and practice it, toward greater human flourishing.*

There are some important things to remember about generosity. Generosity is all about the heart. If your heart is kind, and you give with loving kindness, giving is a holy act. If, however, you give grudgingly, and feel that you are giving only because it is a duty, your generosity is tainted. That is why Eckhart Tolle in his book, *The Power of Now,* wrote, "Who you are is more important than what you do." He gave the example of giving bread to a person in need. There is a difference between the giver giving bread to a person as one human being helping another in need and the giver feeling that he is a superior person and able to help another person who is beneath him.

When we think of generosity, many people believe that it involves money, but generosity involves more than just finances. We can give our time. We can give praise and compliments. We can give flowers. We can give a smile.

How can we be generous in a world of scarcity? To be generous, we have to trust God to give us what we need.

Rabindranath Tagore, Indian poet, Nobel Prize Winner for Literature, wrote:

> *This is my prayer to thee, my lord—strike, strike at the root of penury in my heart.*
> *Give me strength lightly to bear my joys and sorrows,*
> *Give me strength to make my love fruitful in service.*
> *Give me strength never to disown the poor or bend my knees before insolent might.*
> *Give me the strength to raise my mind above trifles.*
> *And give me strength to surrender to thy will with love.*

Tagore's prayer indicates confidence that the Lord will provide for him, and he prays to the Lord not to give him a mentality of poverty, but help him in his service to humankind.

Generosity is a blessing. We know that God himself gave us his only son because he loves us so much, and that Son died on a cross for us. This is the ultimate act of generosity. We are not asked to make such a sacrifice, but we are encouraged to help those who need our help.

Some time ago, I attended a beautiful wedding in Dallas, Texas. A close relative of my son-in-law was getting married, and it was the turn of the father of the bride to speak. At his daughter's wedding, Amal exhorted the bride and groom to remember to help people who are less fortunate than themselves, and I thought, "What a beautiful and unusual speech to give at your daughter's wedding." Amal, incidentally, is part of the Lily Foundation, which has helped, and is still helping disadvantaged youth in India. He is giving for all the right reasons.

This sentiment is echoed by several poets.

In his poem, *Better than Gold*, Abram Joseph Ryan wrote:

> *Better than grandeur, better than gold,*
> *Than rank and titles a thousandfold,*
> *Is a healthy body and a mind at ease,*
> *And simple pleasures that always please.*
> *A heart that can feel for another's woe,*
> *And share his joys with a genial glow;*
> *With sympathies large enough to enfold*
> *All men as brothers, is better than gold.*

As long as humans live in communities, generosity will manifest itself and there will always be people who demonstrate more generosity than others. They will be happier, more fulfilled and will be treasured by societies in which they find themselves.

52 LEADERSHIP

When people live in communities, it is natural that they assume certain roles because they have skills and aptitudes in various areas. And always, someone will emerge as a leader. How do we choose the people who would lead us?

The Center for Management & Organization Effectiveness emphasizes that a good leader should:

- be able to work cooperatively with teams, without worrying too much about being liked.

- have good public-speaking skills.

- be able to efficiently solve operational problems.

- have a hunger to succeed.

- be able and willing to delegate and empower others to make decisions on their own.

- have qualities in common with the people they lead.

One expert on leadership, Kevin Kruse, stressed that authentic leaders must be:

1. Self-aware and genuine. Authentic leaders are self-actualized individuals who are aware of their strengths, their limitations, and their emotions. They also show their real selves to their followers.

2. Mission driven and focused on results. They can put the mission and the goals of the organization ahead of their own self-interest.

3. Able to lead with their heart, not just their minds. They are not afraid to show their emotions, their vulnerability and to connect with their employees.

4. Able to focus on the long-term. They have a goal in mind and do not let short term obstacles keep them from this goal.

However, in real life not everybody adheres to the above principles and might have different concepts of leadership. For example, I attended a leadership course in the East York Board of Education and some participants wanted to demonstrate their leadership qualities to the director. They wanted to show how strong they were by continually belittling other participants. One Supervisor in the same Board wanted to prove how much power she possessed by always flexing her muscles and power-playing in her interactions with the consultants and other employees in the Board offices.

Then there are others like a friend of mine, Karan, who served as vice-principal of summer school one year. A teacher who taught summer school described him as "having the gentleness of a kitten, and the power of a lion." Karan knew what he wanted and was quite firm in his convictions, but his gentle approach led teachers to support him in achieving the goals of the school.

The question arises whether a leader should strive to be a leader, or whether he should be chosen by the people.

Relating to this, Luke chapter 22, verses 24-27 provide some food for thought:

A dispute also arose among them, as to which of them was to be regarded as the greatest.

And he said to them, "The kings of the Gentiles exercise lordship over them, and those in authority over them are called benefactors.

But not so with you. Rather, let the greatest among you become as the youngest, and the leader as one who serves.

For who is the greater, one who reclines at table or one who serves? But I am among you as the one who serves.

This type of leadership is often referred to as *servant leadership*. The leader is regarded as a servant to the will of the people and serves as a facilitator who empowers others to get the task completed.

My brother Dr. Dwarka Ramphal illustrated the concept of servant leadership and the hierarchical nature of leadership by the beatitudes which he termed, *beatific leadership*, in his Ph.D. thesis.

The leader as facilitator is recommended by Lao Tzu, the Chinese philosopher who wrote, "A leader is best when people barely know he exists. When his work is done, his aim fulfilled, they will say: we did it ourselves."

Thus, the good leader will be a mentor, a coach, and a friend who will want the best for you. He will not dictate what's best, but will facilitate the process whereby you come to the understanding of what is the correct choice.

Another quality of the good leader was described by

Napoleon Bonaparte who described a leader as, "...a dealer in hope."

To have hope, you must have faith—faith in your community, faith in your church, and faith in yourselves as leaders in your own destinies.

We are all leaders in some aspects of our lives. As leaders, let us respect and empower the people with whom we work to achieve our mutual goals. You can do this by encouraging the people you are with—at work, in sports, at home—to take pride in their accomplishments and live satisfied lives.

ABOUT THE AUTHOR

Kennard Ramphal started his working life as a pupil teacher at Wales Presbyterian School in 1957. In 1966, he joined the Guyana Defence Force (GDF) as an Officer Cadet and was trained at the Mons Officer Cadet School, in England. On his return to Guyana, he was commissioned as a second lieutenant. During his army career, Ken served in several capacities, including Executive officer in the Engineer Battalion, and ADC to the acting governor general, Sir Edward Luckhoo and the first President of Guyana, His Excellency Arthur Chung.

He graduated from the University of Guyana in 1974, and immigrated to Canada in 1975, where he earned his Masters and Ph.D. degrees at the Ontario Institute for Studies in Education.

Ken taught English and Social Studies in the East York Board of Education, and was the Anti-Racist consultant in the East York Board before joining the Ontario Ministry of Education and Training in 1994 as an education officer. He retired from the Ministry in 1996, and joined the Scarborough Centre for Alternative Studies, where he taught E.S.L, Law and Co-op education.

He retired in 2013, and devoted his time to writing.

In addition to his books, Ken has written several articles on various subjects, including multiculturalism, and the teaching of reading to students who speak the Creole dialect.

His latest book, *THOUGHTS TO MEDITATE ON,* is his eight.

Bibliography

Bell, Jeff, 2011. *Make Belief,* New World Library, Novato, California

Bell, Jeff. *Psychology Today,* January 1, 2016

Canfield, Jack, Hansen, Mark Victor and Newmark, Amy, 2010. *Chicken Soup for the Soul: Think Positive,* Simon and Schuster, Canada

Carlson, Richard. DON'T SWEAT THE SMALL STUFF...and it's all small stuff, 1997. Hyperion, New York

Carnegie, Dale, 1944. *How to Stop Worrying and Start Living,* Pocket Books, New York

Carter-Scott, Cherie, 1998. *IF LIFE is GAME, THESE are the Rules,* Bantam Doubleday Dell Publishing Group, Inc., New York

CBS News, Colorado, November, 2019

Chopra, Deepak, 1994. *The Seven Spiritual Laws of Success,* Amber-Allen Publishing and New World Library, California

Chopra, Deepak, 2004. *The Book of Secrets,* Three Rivers Press, New York

Clinton, Hillary, 2017. *WHAT HAPPENED,* Simon and Schuster, New York, NY.

Daley, Jim, 2019. *The Book of This Day in History,* Publications International Ltd. Illinois

Dennis-Tiwari, Tracey, 2022 *Future Tense: Why*

Anxiety Is Good for You (Even Though It Feels Bad), Piatus, London

Dyer, Wayne, 2001, Secrets for SUCCESS and INNER PEACE, Hay House, Inc., USA

Dyer, Wayne, 2019. *Happiness is the Way,* Hay House, Inc. Carlsbad, California, New York City, London, Sydney, New Delhi

Ehrmann, Max *Desiderata,* 1972, Indiana

Freire, Paulo: Pedagogy of the Oppresssed, 1970, Continuum Internatioal Publishing Group Inc, NY

Fitzgerald, F. Scott. *The Great Gatsby, 2019. The Great Gatsby. Wordsworth Collector's Editions. Ware, England: Wordsworth Editions.*

Garfa FZE, 2024. *Soul*

Krave Website

Gibran, Kahlil, 1923. *The Prophet,* Alfred Knopf, New York

Helmstetter, Shad, 1986. *WHAT TO SAY WHEN YOU TALK TO YOURSELF,* Thorsons, London

Howell, Clinton (ed.) 1970. *Better Than Gold. Thomas Nelson Inc., Nashville, Tenessee,* USA

Kross, Ethan. 2021. *The Voice I Our Head, Why It Matters, and How to Harness It,* Crown

McCaul Smith, Andrew, 2007. *Love Over Scotland*, Anchor, Edinburgh

McGeer, "Johnny's Eight Cow Wife*, Women's Day,* 1965 edition

McGraw, Phillip, 2021. *Self Matters*, Simon & Schuster Source, New

York, NY

Peale, Norman Vincent, 1952. *The Power of Positive Thinking, Prentice Hall Inc., New York*

Pope, Alexander, 1711. *Essay on Criticism,* Published anonymously

Psychology Today, April 3, 2015. Sussex Publishers, New York

Ramphal, Kennard, "My Odyssey," taken from *Roraima: An anthology of poetry from emerging Caribbean Canadian Writers,* Roop Misir, <u>et al,</u> Toronto, Canada, 2011

Reader's Digest, May 2022, Montreal, Canada

Reader's Digest, August 2023, Montreal, Canada

Reader's Digest, November 2023, Montreal, Canada

Shakespeare, William, and John Fletcher, Edited by Eugene M. Waith, 1989, Oxford University Press

Share, December 2024, Vol 46, No. 19, Toronto, Canada

Shaw, George Bernard. *Pygmalion,* 1913

Smith. Christian. *Science of Generosity,* May 2014

Sweet, Derrick, *Healthy Wealthy and Wise,* 2002. The Healthy Wealthy and Wise Corporation, Toronto, Canada

Tagore, Rabindranath. *Gitanjali,* 1913, Macmillan India Ltd., New Delhi, India.

Tolle, Eckhart, 1999. *The Power of Now,* New World Library and Namaste Publishing, California and Vancouver.

Tolle, Eckhart, 2003. Stillness Speaks, New World Library and Namaste Publishing, California and Vancouver.

Watson, Lillian Webster (Editor), 1951. *LIGHT FROM MANY LAMPS,* Simon and Schuster, New York

Webster, Rachel Janison, 2011, Novato, California, New World Library

Wordsworth, William. *Ode: Intimations of Immortality from Recollections of Early Childhood*

Zeland, Vadin, 2003. *Reality Transurfing,* KDP, Amazon Self Publishing

ALSO FROM MIDDLEROAD PUBLISHERS

MiddleRoad | Publishers

www.middleroadpublishers.ca

Making Literature See The Light Of Day

All books available at Amazon worldwide eBook versions available from all eBook channels

Anthology of Brampton
Writers' Guild Authors

OUTSIDE THE WIRE
[Short Stories]
By Michael Joll

PAGES FROM A
NOTEBOOK
[Non-Fiction]
By Ken Puddicombe

PEOPLE OF GUYANA
[Poems]
By Ian McDonald and Peter
Jailall

PERFECT EXECUTION
AND OTHER STORIES
by Michael Joll

PERSONS OF INTEREST
[Short Stories]
By Michael Joll

POEMS FOR MARY
By Ian McDonald

RACING WITH THE RAIN
[a Novel]
By Ken Puddicombe

RAMLALL'S STRANGE
COURTSHIP AND
WEDDING
[Short Stories]

By Kennard Ramphal

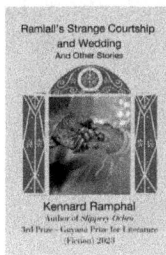

Ramlall's Strange Courtship
and Wedding
And Other Stories

Kennard Ramphal
Author of *Slippery Ochro*
3rd Prize - Guyana Prize for Literature
(Fiction) 2023

RUTHLESS RHYTHMS
[Poems]
By Judith Gelberger

SCALING NEW HEIGHTS
Anthology of Pakaraima
Authors

SLIPPERY OCHRO
[a Novel]
:3rd Prize Guyana Prize For
Literature (Fiction) 2023
By Kennard Ramphal

Slippery OCHRO
-A Novel-

Kennard Ramphal
Author of Seeram's Illusions

THE DARKEST HOURS
[a Novel]
By Michael Joll

THE GARDEN
[Poems]
By Ian McDonald

THE PRICE OF FREEDOM
Bk1
[a novel]
By Judith Gelberger

THE RIVER CROSSING
[Poems and non-Fiction]
By Harry Persaud

SNAPSHOTS OF OUR LIVES
[Anthology]
By Ram Jagessar, Roop Misir and Kennard Ramphal

Snapshots of our Lives

Ram Jagessar
Roop Misir
Kennard Ramphal

TROPICAL SCENES
[Poems]
By Ken Puddicombe

UNFATHOMABLE AND OTHER POEMS
by Ken Puddicombe

WEALTH THROUGH REAL ESTATE INVESTING
[Self-Help]
By Jay Brijpaul

SPARKLES AND KARIM
[a Novel]
By Dave Moores

WINDWARD LEGS
[a Novel]
By Dave Moores

TASTE MY WORDS
[Poems]
By Lisa Freemantle

WITHOUT A WURDUVA LIE
[Short Stories]
By Garry Ferguson

WITNESSES AND OTHER STORIES
By Raymond Holmes

---

www.ingramcontent.com/pod-product-compliance
Lightning Source LLC
Chambersburg PA
CBHW060236050426
42448CB00009B/1462